The Magical Power of
Suru

The Magical Power of
Suru
JAPANESE VERBS MADE EASY

Nobuo Sato

Charles E. Tuttle Company
Rutland, Vermont & Tokyo, Japan

Published by the Charles E. Tuttle Company, Inc.
of Rutland, Vermont & Tokyo, Japan
with editorial offices at
2-6 Suido, 1-chome, Bunkyo-ku, Tokyo 112

LCC Card No. 95-60249
ISBN 0-8048-2025-2

First edition, 1995

Printed in Japan

Contents

Preface

It is my sincere wish that this book will encourage foreign students of the Japanese language who are on the verge of giving up due to the often painful process of memorizing complicated verb conjugations. I also hope to encourage those who are hesitant to start learning the language due to exaggerated rumors concerning the excessive hardship involved in doing so. Now you can approach the study of Japanese in a more relaxed manner, free of verb stress!

Lastly, I wish to thank the Charles E. Tuttle Company for assisting in all publication arrangements, and Lesley Martin for proofreading and editing.

Introduction

Many students of the Japanese language find themselves stumped and frustrated by the complexity and variety of Japanese verbs, their conjugations, and their often ambiguous contexts. The mind-numbing task of memorizing them all is sometimes enough to daunt even the most *ganbarō* student of the language. This book is intended to ease this tremendous burden. How? Via the magical power of *suru*, of course!

The Japanese verb *suru* is roughly equivalent to the English "to do" or "to make." In English, these verbs are sometimes used in combination with various nouns to create verbal idioms or compound verbs. For example, "to do" combined with "laundry" means to wash one's laundry, and "to make" combined with "(a) reservation" means to reserve something in advance. Likewise, the verb *suru* can be combined with not only nouns but adjectives, loanwords, onomatopoeia, and other verbs, as well. *Suru* is thereby capable of creating a wide variety of versatile verbal phrases or compound verbs. And the best part is that students can increase their fluency by relying on just one conjugation pattern! This unique function of *suru* can be a great relief to serious students of the Japanese language. Compound-*suru* verbs are so commonly used that they can virtually replace the majority of regular Japanese verbs, the conjugations of which would otherwise have to be painstakingly memorized one by one.

Here are some examples of noun-*suru* combinations:

junbi-suru 準備する *junbi* (preparation) + *suru*
• to prepare
   *Asu no jugyō o **junbi-shinakereba** narimasen.*
   I must prepare for tomorrow's classes.

yoyaku-suru 予約する *yoyaku* (reservation) + *suru*
• to make a reservation
   ***Yoyaku-shitai** no desu ga.*
   I'd like to make a reservation, please.

These compound-*suru* verbs are undoubtedly familiar to any intermediate student of Japanese. But wait. There's more! Through the magic of *suru*, those pernicious loanwords and onomatopoeia can be easily incorporated into your everyday speech.

memorii-suru メモリーする *memorii* (memorize) + *suru*
• to memorize

*Korera no dōshi no katsuyō o zenbu **memorii-shina-kutemo** yoi to wa ureshii desu ne!*

I'm glad I don't have to memorize all those complicated verb conjugations!

chin-suru チンする *chin* (automatic alarm sound of a microwave oven) + *suru*
• to cook with a microwave oven

*Saikin isogashii node insutanto shokuhin o denshi-renji de **chin-shite imasu.***

I just cook instant food with a microwave oven, since I'm so busy these days.

Additionally, almost all adjectives can be combined with *suru*, as in the following examples. Note that adjectives end with *i* when modifying nouns. When combined with *suru*, however, the final *i* becomes *ku*, as in the following examples:

usuku-suru 薄くする *usui* (thin) + *suru*
• to make thin

*Tsugi no pankēki wa chotto **usuku-shite** kudasai.*

Make the next pancake a little thinner.

tanoshiku-suru 楽しくする *tanoshii* (pleasant, fun) + *suru*
• to make pleasant or fun

*Moshi Amaria ga itara, pātii o **tanoshiku-shite** kureru to omoimasu ne!*

If Amalia's here, she's sure to make the party fun!

This way of using *suru* has recently become so fashionable in contemporary Japanese that new words are being created almost daily. It's an amusing and playful aspect of a language with a reputation for its stiff formalities.

asashan-suru アサシャンする *asashan* (morning shampoo) + *suru*
• to shampoo in the morning

tabako-suru タバコする *tabako* (tobacco) + *suru*
• to smoke, hence to take a rest

hyakutōban-suru 110番する *hyakutōban* (number 110) + *suru*
• to call the police
*Note that in a similar way, *hyakujūkyūban* (119) + *suru* can indicate a call to the emergency number, *ichi-rei-yon-suru* (104) to information, *ichi-ichi-roku-suru* (116) to telephone repair, *ichi-nana-nana-suru* (177) to obtain a weather forecast, etc. See the telephone directory for further details.

In this book you will find the various usages above demonstrated at greater length. The following section presents an easy-to-understand explanation of *suru* and its conjugation patterns. Refer to it throughout the book as you encounter new or unfamiliar *suru* conjugations.

The Magical Power of Suru is divided into twelve chapters. Ten of these are organized according to situations a foreigner coming to Japan might encounter. This topical treatment is not intended as an informational guide for the newcomer to Japan, but to offer the vocabulary one needs to navigate through such situations while applying *suru* verbs. The last two chapters deal specifically with other types of compound-*suru* verbs; that is, loanwords and onomatopoeiac words and expressions.

Each chapter is presented in four sections. "The Situation" sets the scenario, introducing possible usages of *suru* in a particular circumstance, be it your initial arrival in Japan, a discussion on politics, or the use of loanwords in everyday speech. Next is a "Sample Dialogue" section showcasing some of the most useful or common verbs pertinent to the situation. The verbs featured in the dialogues are given individual attention in the section titled "Structures and Synonyms." Here the reader can further examine the makeup of each *suru* verb in the dialogue, and compare it to other synonymous verbs. The last segment of each chapter, "For Further Study," gives similar treatment to a few other verbs considered important to the situation. Finally, an appendix offers an alphabetical list of all featured compound-*suru* verbs for the reader's quick reference.

In short, this book saves the student of Japanese a lot of unnecessary toil and precious time spent mastering unfathomable Japanese verbs and getting accustomed to their ever-changing forms in a variety of contexts. Now you can have it all in one simple, easy-to-use package: the magical power of *suru*!

Suru Conjugations

The conjugation pattern below can be applied to all other compound-*suru* verbs. Let's examine the pattern using the verb *setsumei-suru*. For further clarification of the nuances of each *suru* conjugation, please refer to the sample sentences following the definitions. In most cases, the corresponding negative forms are included. The conjugations in parenthesis are polite forms of the verb.

setsumei-suru 説明する *setsumei* (explanation) + *suru* (to do)
• to explain

su + ru
(a) Denotes the plain, sentence-ending form of the verb.
   *Sensei wa sono riyū o seito ni **setsumei-suru (-shimasu** or **-itashimasu**).*
   The teacher explains the reason to the student.

(b) Denotes the continuation of a sentence or linkage with nouns, pronouns, or other classes of words.

> *Sono riyū o seito ni **setsumei-suru** hito wa sensei desu.*
>
> The person who explains the reason to the student is the teacher.

(c) Denotes probability, possibility, uncertainty, or doubt by adding *darō,* corresponding to "should" or "would" in English.

> *Sensei wa sono riyū o seito ni **setsumei-suru darō**.*
>
> The teacher should explain the reason to the student.

shi + nai

Denotes negation, conveying the idea of denying something or saying no.

> *Sensei wa sono riyū o seito ni **setsumei-shinai (-shimasen)**.*
>
> The teacher does not explain the reason to the student.

shi + ta

Denotes an action or state that is completed at, or during, a definite period of time in the past; the past tense. The negative form is *setsumei-shinakatta (-shimasen deshita)*.

> *Sensei wa sono riyū o **setsumei-shita (-shimashita)**.*
>
> The teacher explained the reason to the student.

sa + seru

Denotes causation, conveying the idea of letting or making someone do something. The negative form is *setsumei-sasenai (-sasemasen)*.

> *Sensei wa seito ni sono riyū o setsumei-saseru (-sasemasu)*.

The teacher lets a student explain the reason.

sa + reru

(a) Denotes the passive voice, conveying the idea of receiving an action or of an action being done by someone or something. The negative form is *setsumei-sarenai (-saremasen)* .

> *Sono riyū wa seito ni yori setsumei-sareru (-saremasu)*.

The reason is explained by the student.

(b) Denotes respect for the person about whom something is said, resulting in a polite expression.

> *Sensei wa seito ni sono riyū o setsumei-sareru (-saremasu)*.

The teacher explains the reason to the student.

shi + te

(a) Denotes present participle (-ing), forming the progressive tense by adding *iru*. The negative form is *setsumei-shite inai (-shite imasen)* .

> *Sensei wa sono riyū o seito ni setsumei-shite iru (-shite imasu or -shite orimasu)*.

The teacher is explaining the reason to the student.

(b) Denotes present participle construction, corresponding to a clause.

Sensei wa sono riyū o seito ni setsumei-shite, shorui o watashita.

Explaining the reason to the student, the teacher handed the document to him.

(c) Denotes a request or polite command when combined with the fixed form of *kudasai*. The negative form is *setsumei-shinaide kudasai*.

Sono riyū o setsumei-shite kudasai.

Please explain the reason.

shi + tai

Denotes a wish or desire, conveying the idea of wanting to do something. The negative form is *setsumei-shitakunai (-shitaku arimasen).*

Sensei wa sono riyū o seito ni setsumei-shitai (-shitai desu).

The teacher wants to explain the reason to the student.

shi + nagara

Denotes the idea of doing two (or more) things simultaneously, as in "during the time that," "at the same time," or "while."

Sensei wa sono riyū o seito ni setsumei-shinagara, kokuban ni e o kaku (kakimasu).

The teacher draws a picture on the blackboard while he explains the reason to the student.

su + re

Denotes supposition or condition in conjunction with the

particle *ba*, often with *moshi* placed at the beginning of a sentence, corresponding to the "if" clause in English. The negative form is ***setsumei-shinakereba***.

> *Moshi sensei ga sono riyū o seito ni **setsumei-sureba**, mondai wa okoranai darō.*
>
> There will be no problem if the teacher explains the reason to the student.

se + yo

Denotes the imperative mood, conveying the idea of ordering someone to do something; interchangeable with ***shi + ro***, which is often used in spoken Japanese. The negative form is ***setsumei-suruna (-shinaide** kudasai)* .

> *Sono riyū o **setsumei-seyo (-shiro)**.*
>
> Explain the reason.

*Note that this is a real command form and should not be used in normal conversations. If you want to ask someone to do something, always use the *shi + te* form plus *kudasai*.

dekiru

Denotes the potential form of *suru;* namely, the ability to do something. The negative form is ***setsumei-dekinai (-dekimasen)***.

*Although *dekiru* is used more often as a stand-alone verb, compounds with *dekiru* are hyphenated in this book to indicate its usage as the potential form of *suru*.

> *Sensei wa sono riyū o seito ni **setsumei-dekiru (-dekimasu)**.*
>
> The teacher can explain the reason to the student.

1

Entering Japan

THE SITUATION

To legally enter Japan you must deal with the necessary formalities, such as immigration papers, customs declaration, and quarantine inspection. Most officials normally speak some English, but don't miss this opportunity to practice. Don't miss out on any chances to speak Japanese—even before you *chakuriku-suru* (land) at the airport!

Of course, if you *mitsunyūkoku-suru* (enter illegally) into Japan, compound-*suru* verbs are still applicable should you have to *mikkō-suru* (stow away), or *tōsō-suru* (escape, run away). Beware, however, of the tragic fate that awaits illegal entrants. Immigration officials or police may *taiho-suru* (arrest) such individuals, and finally *tsuihō-suru* (expel, deport), or even *kankin-suru* (imprison) them.

But let's go back to the average situation of entering Japan. The immigration officers' main job is to *kensa-suru* (to check, to examine). The officer examines your passport and visa. If they are not in order, he may *kyohi-suru* (refuse) your entry. If they are in order, he will *shōnin-suru* (admit) you and *natsuin-suru* (stamp) your passport. Following this procedure, you must *tsūkan-suru* (clear) your personal effects. If you try to *mitsuyu-suru* (smuggle) narcotics or guns, police dogs will *hakken-suru* (discover) them without fail.

If you have two kilograms of gold bars, for example, you must *shinkoku-suru* (declare) them according to import laws, and the customs officer will *kazei-suru* (impose a tax) on them accordingly.

If you unfortunately suffer from cholera or yellow fever, the quarantine officer will *shōdoku-suru* (sterilize) all your belongings and may *kakuri-suru* (isolate) you. Also, if you *hatsunetsu-suru* (are feverish) or *geri-suru* (have diarrhea), then the doctor in charge will *shinsatsu-suru* (examine) you carefully. If there are no problems, customs will *kyoka-suru* (permit) you to enter Japan legally.

But don't jump into a taxi or limousine bus just yet. First, *ryōgae-suru* (change money) at the bank inside the airport. As a Japanese proverb says, *Isogaba maware* (Make haste slowly)!

DIALOGUE

TOURIST: *Sumimasen ga, nimotsu wa doko de **kensa-suru** no desu ka?*
Excuse me, but where do you check our baggage?

CUSTOMS OFFICIAL: *Koko desu. Nanika **shinkoku-suru** mono wa arimasu ka?*
Right here. Is there anything to declare?

TOURIST: *Rorekkusu no kin dokei o motte imasu ga.*
I have a gold Rolex watch.

CUSTOMS OFFICIAL: *Kore ni wa kazei saremasu yo. Ano madoguchi de **nōzei-shite** kudasai.*
This article is taxed. Please pay the tax at the window over there.

Finishing the customs clearance, the tourist moves to the immigration counter.

IMMIGRATION OFFICIAL: *Pasupōto o **teiji-shite** kudasai.*
Please show your passport.

TOURIST: *Hai, dōzo.*
Yes, sure.

IMMIGRATION OFFICIAL: *Donna mokuteki de **rainichi-sare-mashita** ka?*

What is your purpose for visiting Japan?

TOURIST: *Kankō-suru/Shigoto-suru* tame ni *rainichi-shimashita.*
I came to sightsee/to work.

IMMIGRATION OFFICIAL: *Nan nichi kan/Nan kagetsu kan* **taizai-shimasu** *ka?*
How many days/How many months are you staying?

TOURIST: *Itsuka kan/kyūkagestu kan no taizai o* **yotei-shite imasu.**
I plan a five-day stay/a nine-month stay.

IMMIGRATION OFFICIAL: *Nihon de* **shigoto-suru** *toki wa, kyoka ga hitsuyō desu. Rōdō kyokasho o* **shutoku-shite imasu** *ka?*
In order to work in Japan, you need a permit. Have you obtained a work permit?

TOURIST: *Hai, achira no Nihon taishikan de* **hakkō-shite moraimashita.**
Yes, it was issued by the Japanese Embassy over there.

IMMIGRATION OFFICIAL: *Chotto sore o* **haiken-dekimasu** *ka?*
Can I see it for a moment?

TOURIST: *Hai, kore desu.*
Yes, here it is.

IMMIGRATION OFFICIAL: *Donna shigoto ni **jūji-shite imasu** ka?*
What kind of business are you engaged in?

TOURIST: *Konpyūtā o **yunyū-shite**, Nihon de **hanbai-shimasu**. Kono biza de **nyūkoku-dekimasu** ka?*
I import computers and sell them in Japan. Can I enter your country with this visa?

IMMIGRATION OFFICIAL: *Mondai wa arimasen ga, moyori no shiyakusho de sugu gaikokujin tōroku o shite kudasai. Tsugi no kata dōzo*
No problem, but please complete your alien registration soon at the nearest city office. Next person, please.

STRUCTURES AND SYNONYMS

teiji-suru 提示する *teiji* (indication, show) + *suru*
• to show, to indicate, to exhibit
Compare with *miseru* 見せる to show
*Toranku no nakami o **misete** kudasai.*
Please show me the contents of your baggage.

haiken-suru 拝見する *haiken* (look, inspection) + *suru*
• to look, to inspect

Compare with *miru* 見る to see, look; *shiraberu* 調べ
る to inspect, to check
*Chotto pasupōto o **mitai** no desu ga.*
I'd like to see your passport for a minute.

rainichi-suru 来日する *rainichi* (come to Japan) + *suru*
• to come to Japan
   Nichi 日 is the abbreviation for Japan.
   Compare with *Nihon ni kuru* 日本にくる to come to
   Japan; *hōnichi-suru* 訪日する to visit Japan
   *Kare wa kyonen san kai **hōnichi-shimashita**.*
   Last year he visited Japan three times.

kankō-suru 観光する *kankō* (sightseeing) + *suru*
• to see the sights
   Compare with *ryokō-suru* 旅行する to travel, to tour,
   to make a journey
   *Amerika o san shūkan **ryokō-shimasu**.*
   I'll travel in America for three weeks.

shigoto-suru 仕事する *shigoto* (work, job, task) + *suru*
• to work, to do one's job, to do business
   Compare with *hataraku* 働く to work
   *Chichi wa maiban jū-ji made **hatarakimasu**.*
   Dad works until ten every night.

taizai-suru 滞在する *taizai* (stay, sojourn) + *suru*
• to stay, to sojourn, to remain

Compare with *todomaru* 留まる to stay, to remain, to abide, to stand still
*Pari ni itsuka kan **todomaranakereba** narimasen deshita.*
I had to stay in Paris for five days.

yotei-suru 予定する *yotei* (schedule, plan, program) + *suru*
• to be scheduled, to plan, to intend
Compare with *tsumoridearu* 積もりである to intend, to plan
*Kare wa daigaku ni yuku **tsumori** datta.*
He intended to go to college.

shutoku-suru 取得する *shutoku* (acquisition) + *suru*
• to acquire, to gain, to obtain
Compare with *eru* 得る to get; *morau* 貰う to receive, to get
*Biza o **morau** ni wa, ryōjikan ni shuttō-shinakereba narimasen.*
In order to get a visa, you must show yourself to the consulate.

jūji-suru 従事する *jūji* (occupation, engagement) + *suru*
• to be occupied in, to be engaged in
Compare with *tsuku* 就く to engage in, to set to work
*Kare wa kimatta shigoto ni **tsuita** koto ga arimasen.*
He has never been engaged in any fixed job.

yunyū-suru 輸入する *yunyū* (import) + *suru*
• to import

hanbai-suru 販売する *hanbai* (sales) + *suru*
• to sell
    Compare with *uru* 売る to sell
    Kono sērusuman wa kongetsu wa kuruma o nijū dai
    urimashita.
    This salesman sold twenty cars this month.

hakkō-suru 発行する *hakkō* (issuance, publication) +
suru
• to issue, to publish
    Compare with *hakkyū-suru* 発給する to issue
    *Hakkyū-suru is specific and suitable for official documents like
    passports and visas, while *hakkō-suru* is widely applicable to
    various kinds of documents, including but not limited to official
    ones.
    Ryōjikan wa kare ni eijū biza o ***hakkyū-shita***.
    The consulate issued him a permanent visa.

nyūkoku-suru 入国する *nyūkoku* (into a country) + *suru*
• to enter a country
    Compare with *hairu* 入る to enter
    Furansu kara Doitsu ni ***hairimashita***.
    I entered Germany from France.

kensa-suru 検査する *kensa* (inspection, examination, test) + *suru*
- to inspect, to test, to examine
     Compare with *shiraberu* 調べる to inspect, to check
     *Keikan wa unten menkyoshō o **shirabeta**.*
     The policeman examined my driver's license.

shinkoku-suru 申告する *shinkoku* (declaration) + *suru*
- to declare
     Compare with *mōshi deru* 申し出る to declare
     *Kare wa kin no tokei o **mōshi deta**.*
     He declared a gold watch.

kazei-suru 課税する *kazei* (taxation) + *suru*
- to impose a tax, to tax
     Compare with *kakeru* 掛ける to impose
     *Tōkyoku ga kin no tokei ni hyaku doru zeikin o **kakemashita**.*
     The authorities imposed a hundred-dollar tax on my gold watch.

nōzei-suru 納税する *nōzei* (payment of tax) + *suru*
- to pay taxes
     Compare with *shiharau* 支払う to pay
     *Kare wa hyaku doru no zeikin o **shiharatta**.*
     He paid a hundred dollars in tax.

FOR FURTHER STUDY

tokō-suru 渡航する *tokō* (travel by sea, sail) + *suru*
• to travel by sea, to make a voyage, to sail for

> *Kanojo no sofu wa gojū nen mae ni shigoto de Amerika ni **tokō-shimashita**.*
> Her grandfather sailed to America for business 50 years ago.

tobei-suru 渡米する *tobei* (voyage, travel to America) + *suru*
• to make a voyage to America, to travel to America

> **Bei* 米 is the abbreviation for *Beikoku* 米国 or America.
> *Nihon no sōri daijin ga tsūshō mondai o tōgi-suru tame **tobei-suru** yotei desu.*
> Japan's prime minister is scheduled to travel to America to discuss trade issues.

gizō-suru 偽造する *gizō* (forgery, fabrication) + *suru*
• to forge, to fabricate

> *Kono pasupōto wa Honkon de **gizō-sareta**.*
> This passport was forged in Hong Kong.

gaitō-suru 該当する *gaitō* (applicability) + *suru*
• to be applicable, to fall under

> *Kono ken wa iminhō dai-go jō ni **gaitō-suru**.*
> This case falls under Article 5 of the Immigration Law.

2

Getting Settled

THE SITUATION

Upon arrival at your hotel, the doorman will *aisatsu-suru* (greet) you. If you look rich or beautiful enough, he might even smile and add an extra polite tone to his greeting. Otherwise, he might *shitsumon-suru* (question) you as to what your business is. And after he does *kakunin-suru* (confirm) that you are in fact rich enough, his attitude towards you may suddenly *henka-suru* (change). How might he be of service to you?!

Hotels are used for many different purposes, and Japanese hotels are no exception. Some people use a hotel in order to *kaisai-suru* (hold) a party, and others use it to *furin-suru* (indulge in an illicit affair). The traditional synonym for this recently created verb is *uwaki-suru* (be inconstant, be unfaithful). If you are talking to old folks here, the traditional verb is more appropriate and, coincidentally, is an easy-to-conjugate *suru* verb as well.

At the counter, the hotel manager will *yōkyū-suru* (request) that you *kichō-suru* (register) in the visitors' book. If you have something valuable, you are kindly requested to *hokan-suru* (keep) it in the hotel safe. This should then *kanryō-suru* (complete) all your check-in procedures.

Now, you can *hotto-suru* (give a sigh of relief). Go to your room and *kyūkei-suru* (take a rest) or *nyūyoku-suru* (take a bath). If you are not tired, you can *gaishutsu-suru* (go out) and *sanpo-suru* (take a walk) in order to *kengaku-suru* (take a look) around town.

When you have shirts to *sentaku-suru* (wash) or suits to *doraikuriiningu-suru* (dry clean), you can *denwa-suru* (telephone) the front desk. When you get hungry and want to *shokuji-suru* (dine, have a meal), you can just *chakuseki-suru* (sit down) in a cozy corner of the hotel restaurant and *chūmon-suru* (order) your favorite dish. Do you want to have a steak? Eat it at home, not in Japan. It is terribly expensive. *Gō ni irite wa, gō ni shitagae* (When in Rome, do as the Romans). You should try some typical Japanese food.

After dinner, what would you like to do? Want to go to a night club? Well, perhaps after your long flight, you had better *shōtō-suru* (turn off the light) and *shūshin-suru* (go to bed).

Oyasumi nasai! (Good night!)

DIALOGUE

MARY: *Nyūyōku de **yoyaku-shita** Merii Jakuson desu ga.*
I'm Mary Jackson who made reservations in New York.

HOTEL RECEPTIONIST: *Chotto pasupōto o **haishaku-dekimasu** ka? Ima konpyūtā de **chekku-shimasu**.*
May I see your passport for a moment? I'll check it with our computer.

MARY: *Hai, dōzo. Asoko no robii de **taiki-shite imasu** yo.*
Sure. I'll be waiting in the lobby over there.

HOTEL RECEPTIONIST: *Yoyaku o **kakunin-shitara** pejingu-shimasu node.*
After confirming your reservation, I'll page you.

A few minutes pass. Mary is paged and returns to the reception desk.

HOTEL RECEPTIONIST: *Onamae wa chōbo ni tashika ni **kiroku-sarete imashita**. Wakariyasui onamae desu node sugu **hakken-dekimashita**.*
Your name was in fact registered in our book. It's an easy name, so I was able to find it immediately.

MARY: *Yokatta. Kore de **anshin-shimashita**. Shiranai tochi de hoteru o sagasu no wa taihen desu kara ne.*

Great. I feel relieved. It's so hard to find a hotel in places one doesn't know.

HOTEL RECEPTIONIST: *Daijōbu desu yo. Yoyaku ga chōbo ni nai toki ni wa, hoka no hoteru ni **shōkai-itashimasu** kara.*
It's no problem. In the event your reservation couldn't be found in the book, we would introduce you to another hotel.

MARY: *Sō desu ka?*
Is that so?

HOTEL RECEPTIONIST: *Kono chōbo ni onamae to jūsho o **kinyū-shite** kara koko ni **shomei-shite** kudasai.*
Please sign here after filling in your name and address.

MARY: *Kichōhin o **hokan-shite** moraitai no desu ga.*
I would like you to keep my valuables.

HOTEL RECEPTIONIST: *Wakarimashita. Kono fukuro ni irete, **fūin-shite** kudasai. Kagi o **funshitsu-shinai** yō ni shite kudasai. Ima bōi ni heya made **annai-sasemasu.***
Very well. Put them into this bag and seal it. Please be careful not to lose your key. I'll have a bellhop guide you to your room now.

MARY: *Dōmo arigatō. Ano, jibun no heya de **shokuji-dekimasu** ka?*

Thanks. Oh, can I eat in my room?

HOTEL RECEPTIONIST: *Hai, dekimasu. Menyū ya sābisu jikan wa heya no annaisho ni **kisai-sarete imasu**. Okonomi no ryōri o **sentaku-sarete**, kauntā ni **denwa-shite** kudasai.*

Yes, you can. The menu and service times are printed in the guidebook in your room. Please select the desired dishes and phone room service.

MARY: *Hai, wakarimashita. Arigatō gozaimashita.*

I see. Thank you.

STRUCTURES AND SYNONYMS

yoyaku-suru 予約する *yoyaku* (reservation) + *suru*

• to make reservations, to reserve

Compare with *toru* 取る to reserve, to take

*Toru literally means "to take," but in this case it is the shortened form of *yoyaku o toru* (to make a reservation).

*Ryokōsha wa Pari no hoteru o **totte** kureta.*

The travel agency made a hotel reservation in Paris for me.

haishaku-suru 拝借する *haishaku* (borrow) + *suru*

• to borrow

Compare with *kariru* 借りる to borrow, to rent
Ryokō no toki wa itsumo kuruma o karimasu.
When I travel, I always rent a car.

chekku-suru チェックする *chekku* (check) + *suru*
• to check, to examine, to inspect
Compare with *shiraberu* 調べる to check, to investigate
Kachō wa keiyakusho o chūibukaku shirabeta.
The manager carefully checked the contract.

taiki-suru 待機する *taiki* (wait) + *suru*
• to wait
Compare with *matsu* 待つ to wait for
Ōsetsuma de shibaraku o machi kudasai.
Please wait a moment in the drawing room.

kakunin-suru 確認する *kakunin* (confirmation) + *suru*
• to confirm
Compare with *tashikameru* 確かめる to confirm
Shashō ni tōchaku jikan o tashikamemashita.
I confirmed the arrival time with the conductor.

peijingu-suru ページングする *peijingu* (paging) + *suru*
• to page
Compare with *yobidasu* 呼び出す to page, to call out
Osaka no Yamada-san o yobidashite kudasai.
Please page Mr. Yamada from Osaka.

kiroku-suru 記録する *kiroku* (registration) + *suru*
- to record, to register
    Compare with *kakitomeru* 書き留める to take note, to jot down, to record
    *Kare no namae wa nagai node, techō ni **kakitome-mashita***.
    His name is so long that I jotted it down in my notebook.

hakken-suru 発見する *hakken* (discovery, finding) + *suru*
- to discover, to find out
    Compare with *mitsukeru* 見つける to find, to discover
    *Chōsadan wa atarashii kin kōmyaku o **mitsukema-shita***.
    The survey team discovered a new lode of gold-ore.

anshin-suru 安心する *anshin* (peace of mind, relief) + *suru*
- to feel relieved, to have peace of mind
    Compare with *hotto-suru* ほっとする to feel relieved
    *Sore o kiite **hotto-shimashita** yo.*
    I feel relieved to hear that.

shōkai-suru 紹介する *shōkai* (introduction) + *suru*
- to introduce
    Compare with *hikiawaseru* 引き合わせる to introduce, to present

*Sakuya watashi no imōto o tomodachi ni **hikiawaseta***.
Last night I introduced my sister to a friend of mine.

kinyū-suru 記入する *kinyū* (jot down, fill in) + suru
• to jot down, to fill in
Compare with *kaki ireru* 書き入れる to jot down, to write in
*Koko wa namae o **kaki ireru** ran desu*.
This is the column in which you write your name.

shomei-suru 署名する *shomei* (signature) + *suru*
• to sign
Compare with *sain-suru* サインする to sign
*Shachō wa keiyakusho ni **sain-shinakatta***.
The president did not sign the contract.

hokan-suru 保管する *hokan* (deposit, storage) + *suru*
• to deposit, to store, to keep
Compare with *azukeru* 預ける to deposit, to entrust
*Kinko ni kichōhin o **azuketai** no desu ga*.
I'd like to deposit my valuables in the safe.

fūin-suru 封印する *fūin* (seal, stamp) + *suru*
• to seal
Compare with *fū o suru* 封をする to seal
*Kanojo wa tegami no **fū o shinaide** dashimashita*.
She posted her letter without sealing it.

funshitsu-suru 紛失する *funshitsu* (loss) + *suru*
* to be lost, to lose

  Compare with *nakusu* 無くす to lose, to go missing;
  nakunaru 無くなる to be lost

  *Watashi no heya kara tokei ga **nakunarimashita**.*
  My watch is missing from my room.

annai-suru 案内する *annai* (guidance, advice) + *suru*
* to guide, to lead

  Compare with *tebiki-suru* 手引きする to guide, to
  introduce

  *Shōnin wa watashi o mise no naka ni **tebiki-shiyō** to
  shite imasu.*
  The merchant is trying to lead me into his shop.

shokuji-suru 食事する *shokuji* (meal) + *suru*
* to eat, to have a meal

  Compare with *taberu* 食べる to eat

  ***Tabeta** chokugo ni oyoide wa ikemasen.*
  You should not swim immediately after eating.

kisai-suru 記載する *kisai* (description, entry) + *suru*
* to note, to enter, to record

  Compare with *noseru* 載せる to record, to print

  *Tōkyoku wa kare no namae o meibo ni **nosemasen**
  deshita.*
  The authorities did not put his name on the list.

sentaku-suru 洗濯する *sentaku* (laundry, wash) + *suru*
* to wash, to launder
  Compare with *arau* 洗う to wash
  *Haha wa watashi no kutsushita o **aratte imasu***.
  My mother is washing my socks.

denwa-suru 電話する *denwa* (telephone) + *suru*
* to telephone
  Compare with *denwa o kakeru* 電話を掛ける to make a phone call
  *Sugu byōin ni denwa o **kakete** kudasai*.
  Please call the hospital immediately.

FOR FURTHER STUDY

nyūyoku-suru 入浴する *nyūyoku* (bath) + *suru*
* to take a bath or shower, to bathe
  ***Nyūyoku-suru** toki wa, yokushitsu no doa o shimete kudasai*.
  Please shut the door of the bathroom when you take a bath.

shūyō-suru 収容する *shūyō* (accommodation, housing) + *suru*
* to accommodate, to house
  *Kono hoteru wa nannin **shūyō-dekimasu** ka?*
  How many people can this hotel accomodate?

seisan-suru 精算する *seisan* (settlement of account) + *suru*

• to settle an account

*Hoteru dai wa jū-ji made ni **seisan-shite** kudasai.*
Please settle the hotel charges by ten o'clock.

chekkuauto-suru チェックアウトする *chekkuauto* (check-out) + *suru*

• to check out

***Chekkuauto-suru** toki, kagi o henkyaku-shite kudasai.*
When you check out, please return your key.

3

Shopping

THE SITUATION

All consumers naturally *kibō-suru* (hope) to be able to *kōnyū-suru* (purchase) items at low prices. Likewise, all retailers *kibō-suru* to *hanbai-suru* (sell) their merchandise at high prices. Unfortunately, every consumer has a limited budget. When your budget is too tight, you must either *shakkin-suru* (borrow money, obtain a loan) or simply *gaman-suru* (be patient) and *chokin-suru* (save money) till you have enough. The last resort is to *dannen-suru* (to give up, abandon) hope.

Of course, one way around budget limitations is to *yōkyū-suru* (request, demand) a discount. If you can skillfully *kōshō-suru* (negotiate), a retailer will normally *yōnin-suru* (accept) some discount. However, if a merchant gives too big of a discount, you must *chūi-suru* (be careful). Such merchandise may have serious defects. As a result, you might actually *son-suru* (suffer a loss). An unscrupulous merchant may also *tsuika-suru* (add) some amount to the actual price, knowing that you will *yōkyū-suru* (demand) a discount.

In some cases, merchants will *nebiki-suru* (give a discount) when you *kōnyū-suru* (purchase) two or three pieces of the same item or even of different items. For such business transactions, don't forget to *keisan-suru* (calculate) the final amount you are to pay. If you buy several items at the same time, you can *gōkei-suru* (total) the prices in a number of ways. If you buy two items, you should *tashizan-suru* (add) the prices. If you buy several of the same item, *kakezan-suru* (multiply) the price by the number you want to buy. If you want to know the price per unit of a bulk item, *warizan-suru* (divide) the total price by the number you want to buy. When everything is set, you can go ahead and give your money to a clerk. In order to give you change, he will *hikizan-suru* (deduct, subtract) the total from the amount of money you give him.

In a foreign country most people take back souvenirs for their families or friends. Should you find yourself *tōwaku-suru* (perplexed) as to what to buy, you might want to *sōdan-suru* (consult) with a sales clerk. They will *jogen-suru* (advise) you and *suisen-suru* (recommend) something appropriate. You need only *kōryo-suru* (consider) the particular interest or taste of the person in question or the limit of your budget, and *sentaku-suru* (choose) one. Don't worry if you can't make up your mind! If you end up with so many presents that you can't *keitai-suru* (carry) them, most stores will *haitatsu-suru* (deliver) them to your home address or hotel.

DIALOGUE

SHOPPER: *Chotto sumimasen. Asoko ni **tenji-shite iru** rajikase wa ikura desu ka?*
Excuse me. How much is that radio-cassette player you're displaying?

SALES CLERK: *Sore wa ichiman kyūsen en de utte imasu yo.*
That one's on sale for nineteen thousand yen.

SHOPPER: *Are de FM hōsō wa **jushin-dekimasu** ka? Batterii de **sadō-shimasu** ka?*
Can I receive FM broadcasting with it? Does it work on batteries?

SALES CLERK: *Dochira mo daijōbu desu. Jibun de **tesuto-shite** mite kudasai.*
Both are OK. Please test it and see for yourself.

SHOPPER: *Kono tsumami o **kaiten-suru** to **sadō-suru** no desu ka?*
Do I turn this knob to work it?

SALES CLERK: *Sono mae ni konsento ni **setsuzoku-shite** kudasai.*

Before that, please connect it to the outlet.

SHOPPER: *Sō desu ka. FM ni **henkō-suru** ni wa dō suru no desu ka?*
I see. What do I do to change it to FM?

SALES CLERK: *Kono setsumeisho o mite **sōsa-shite** kuremasen ka?*
Would you please look at this manual and operate it accordingly?

After examining the merchandise, the shopper comes to a decision.

SHOPPER: *Nedan no wari ni, iroiro na kinō ga **sōbi-sarete imasu** node, kore o **kōnyū-suru** koto ni **ketteishimashita**.*
For the price, it's well equipped with lots of different functions, so I've decided to purchase it.

SALES CLERK: *Arigatō gozaimasu. Ima sugu **hōsō-sasemasu**.*
Thank you. I'll have it wrapped up right away.

SHOPPER: *Tokoro de, dono kurai **nebiki-dekimasu** ka?*
By the way, how much can you discount it for?

SALES CLERK: *Juppāsento **nebiki-itashimasu**. Sore ijō no nebiki de wa **hanbai-dekimasen**.*

We'll discount ten percent. We're unable to sell it at a higher discount.

SHOPPER: *Niman en o **chōka-shimasu** ka? Kingaku o **keisan-shite** mite kudasai.*
Does it go over twenty thousand yen? Would you try to calculate the amount, please?

SALES CLERK: *Niman en o nihyaku en **chōka-shimasu** ga, anata no yosan o **kōryo-shite**, niman en chōdo ni **benkyō-itashimashō**.*
It goes over twenty thousand by two hundred yen, but considering your budget, we'll cut the price down to just twenty thousand yen.

SHOPPER: *Ah, sore wa dōmo. Hai, niman en desu. Hoteru made **haitatsu-shite** kudasai.*
Oh, thank you. Here is twenty-thousand yen. Can you deliver it to my hotel?

SALES CLERK: *Sumimasen ga, hitode ga chotto **fusoku-shite imasu** node, hoteru made **haitatsu-dekimasen**.*
I'm sorry, but we're a little short-handed, so we can't deliver it to your hotel.

SHOPPER: *Zannen desu ne. **Koshō-shitara**, doko de **shūri-dekimasu ka**?*
That's too bad. If something goes wrong with it, where can I have it repaired?

SALES CLERK: *Hoshōsho o **hakkō-shimashita**. **Koshō-shi-**
***tara**, kono sābisu sutēshon de **shūri-shite** moratte
kudasai. O-kaiage dōmo arigatō gozaimashita.*
We've issued you a warranty card. If something
goes wrong, please have it repaired at this service
station. Thank you for your purchase.

STRUCTURES AND SYNONYMS

tenji-suru 展示する *tenji* (display, exhibition) + *suru*
- to display, to exhibit
  Compare with *kōkai-suru* 公開する to open to the
  public, to display
  *Kono furui shiro wa ippan ni **kokai-saremasen**.*
  This old castle is not open to the public.

jushin-suru 受信する *jushin* (reception of a signal or
message) + *suru*
- to receive a signal or message
  Compare with *hairu* 入る to receive, to catch (literally "to come in")
  *Kono tanpa rajio wa BBC ga yoku **hairimasu**.*
  This short-wave radio receives BBC well.

sadō-suru 作動する *sadō* (functioning, operating, working) + *suru*
- to function, to operate, to work
  Compare with *ugoku* 動く to function, to operate, to
  move

*Kono kuruma wa taiyō enerugii de **ugokimasu**.*
This car is run by solar energy.

tesuto-suru テストする *tesuto* (test, try) + *suru*
• to test, to try
    Compare with *tamesu* 試す to test, to try
    *Watashi wa kono kuruma o ni kai **tameshite** kara kau tsumori desu.*
    I plan to buy this car after testing it twice.

kaiten-suru 回転する *kaiten* (rotation, turn) + *suru*
• to rotate, to revolve, to turn
    Compare with *mawasu* 回す to rotate, to turn
    *Neji o shimeru ni wa hidari ni **mawashite** kudasai.*
    To fasten the screw, turn it to the left.

setsuzoku-suru 接続する *setsuzoku* (link, connection) + *suru*
• to link, to connect, to join
    Compare with *tsunagu* 繋ぐ to link, to connect, to join
    *Daiku wa hashigo o ni hon **tsunaide** yane ni nobotta.*
    The carpenter joined two ladders together to climb up on the roof.

sōsa-suru 操作する *sōsa* (operation, handling) + *suru*
• to operate, to handle, to move
    Compare with *ugokasu* 動かす to operate, to move

*Kono kikai o **ugokasemasu** ka?*
Can you operate this machine?

sōbi-suru 装備する *sōbi* (equipment, feature) + *suru*
• to equip, to be equipped, to feature
Compare with *tsuku* 付く to feature, to be equipped
*Kono yasui kuruma ni wa kassetto ga **tsukimasen**.*
This inexpensive car is not equipped with a cassette player.

kōnyū-suru 購入する *kōnyū* (purchase, acquisition) + *suru*
• to purchase, to acquire, to buy
Compare with *kau* 買う to buy, to purchase
*Wareware wa saikin chūko no uchi o **katta**.*
We recently bought an old house.

kettei-suru 決定する *kettei* (decision, determination) + *suru*
• to decide, to determine
Compare with *kimeru* 決める to decide, to determine
*Kanojo wa hayaku kekkonshiki no hinichi o **kimetai**.*
She wants to decide the date of her wedding ceremony soon.

hōsō-suru 包装する *hōsō* (packing, wrapping) + *suru*
• to pack, to wrap
Compare with *tsutsumu* 包む to pack, to wrap

Sore wa **tsutsumanakute** *mo ii desu.*
You don't have to wrap it.

nebiki-suru 値引きする *nebiki* (discount) + *suru*
• to discount, to deduct from the price
   Compare with *makeru* まける to discount, to lower
   Ano shōnin wa watashi ni **maketa** *koto ga nai.*
   That merchant has never given me any discount.

hanbai-suru 販売する *hanbai* (sale, marketing) + *suru*
• to sell, to market
   Compare with *uru* 売る to sell, to market
   Jinushi wa sono tochi o kesshite **urimasen**.
   The landowner will never sell that land.

keisan-suru 計算する *keisan* (calculation, count) + *suru*
• to calculate, to count
   Compare with *kazoeru* 数える to calculate, to count
   Iinkai wa tōhyōsha no sōsū o **kazoete imasu**.
   The committee is counting the voters' total.

chōka-suru 超過する *chōka* (excess, surplus) + *suru*
• to exceed, to surpass
   Compare with *koeru* 越える to exceed, to surpass
   Kono machi no jinkō wa ichiman nin o **koeta**.
   This town's population exceeds ten thousand.

kōryo-suru 考慮する *kōryo* (consideration) + *suru*
• to consider
    Compare with *kangaeru* 考える to consider, to think
    *Shachō wa shain no koto wa amari **kangaemasen
    deshita.***
    The president did not consider his employees very
    much.

benkyō-suru 勉強する *benkyō* (reduction, discount) +
suru
• to reduce, to discount
    Compare with *makeru* まける to discount, to lower
    *Ano mise wa itsumo **makete** kureru.*
    That store always gives me a discount.

haitatsu-suru 配達する *haitatsu* (delivery) + *suru*
• to deliver
    Compare with *todokeru* 届ける to deliver
    *Kore o hoteru e **todokete** kudasai.*
    Please deliver this to my hotel.

fusoku-suru 不足する *fusoku* (shortage, lack) + *suru*
• to be short, to lack
    Compare with *tarinai* 足りない to be short, to lack
    *Kare wa wakai node, keiken ga **tarinai**.*
    Since he is young, he's lacking in experience.

koshō-suru 故障する *koshō* (damage, a breakdown) + *suru*
• to breakdown, to become out of order
Compare with *kowareru* 毀れる to be broken, to be wrecked
Kono tokei wa kowareteimasu.
This clock is out of order.

shūri-suru 修理する *shūri* (repair, mending) + *suru*
• to repair, to mend
Compare with *naosu* 直す to fix, to repair
*Kare wa jibun de jitensha o **naoshimasu**.*
He fixes his bicycle by himself.

FOR FURTHER STUDY

yasu uri-suru 安売りする *yasu uri* (bargain sale, discount sale) + *suru*
• to sell at a lower price
*Nihon wa subete no seihin o **yasu uri-shite iru**.*
Japan sells all its products at lower prices.

tokubai-suru 特売する *tokubai* (a special sale) + *suru*
• to sell at a special price
*Kono depāto wa natsu no owari ni shibashiba **tokubai-shimasu**.*
At the end of summer, this department store often sells its merchandise at special prices.

hoshō-suru 保証する *hoshō* (warranty, guarantee) + *suru*
• to guarantee

>*Seizō gyōsha wa seihin no hinshitsu o ichi nen kan*
>**hoshō-shimasu.**
>The manufacturer guarantees the quality of the product for one year.

4

Studying Japanese

THE SITUATION

Nowadays a large number of foreigners *rainichi-suru* (come to Japan) in order to *benkyō-suru* (study) Japanese. But in reality, many of these "students" actually come to *shigoto-suru* (work). This is because it's easier to *shutoku-suru* (get) a student visa than a proper work visa. Are you here for the high yen rate rather than an opportunity to learn? No? Good! Then, let's take a closer look at studying in Japan.

There are many language schools all over Japan. First of all you should *shūshū-suru* (collect) a few leaflets from different ones. Carefully *jukudoku-suru* (peruse) your options, and *sentaku-suru* (choose) the best school for your needs. You will have to *kinyū-suru* (fill in) the application form and *yūsō-suru* (mail) it to the school. Often, you must also *sōkin-suru* (remit) the total entrance fee required for your enrollment. Soon you will *juryō-suru* (receive) a document stating that they can *kyoka-suru* (approve) your enrollment. Now you will want to *junbi-suru* (prepare) as quickly as possible. You don't want to miss your first day!

If you haven't visited yet, *chokkō-suru* (go directly) to your new school. On the first day you will be asked to *sanka-suru* (participate) in the opening ceremony. Your participation means you are officially *nyūgaku-suru* (enrolled). Congratulations! Now the real work begins. At home, be sure to *yoshū-suru* (prepare lessons). Classes *kaishi-suru* (begin) the day after the opening ceremony.

In a typical class, the teacher will drill you on how to *hatsuon-suru* (pronounce) Japanese words. You should *mane-suru* (imitate) the teacher's pronunciation. It's OK if you don't get it right away. Teachers normally *hanpuku-suru* (repeat) the pronunciation a few times. Some teachers will *meirei-suru* (order) you to *rōdoku-suru* (read) the textbook. *Kiritsu-suru* (stand up) when you read. When you make a mistake, your teacher will *teisei-suru* (correct) it. If you have to *teishi-suru* (stop) in front of a difficult kanji, your teacher may ask the class if anyone knows how to read it. Hopefully, someone will be able to *hentō-suru* (reply) correctly.

Every day, the teacher will *shiteki-suru* (point out) some new kanji to *gakushū-suru* (learn) or have you *anshō-suru* (memorize) important phrases. If you have a question, don't *chūcho-suru* (hesitate) to *shitsumon-suru* (ask) your teachers. It's their job to *setsumei-suru* (explain) your question in detail for you to fully *rikai-suru* (understand).

When your classes are over, you are free to *gekō-suru* (leave school). But studying doesn't end in the classroom. At home you must *fukushū-suru* (review) what you have learned. Teachers often *shiken-suru* (test), but if you *renshū-suru* (practice) or *benkyō-suru* (study) every night, you will find the tests easy!

With a little effort, you will soon *kanryō-suru* (complete) all your courses and *sotsugyō-suru* (graduate). At the ceremony the school administrator will give you a certificate to *shōmei-suru* (certify) your achievement. *Hokan-suru* (preserve) it carefully. You can *teiji-suru* (show) it when you *shūshoku-suru* (get a job)!

DIALOGUE

STUDENT: *Nihongo ga **benkyō-shitai** node, kono gakkō ni **nyūgaku-shitai** no desu ga.*
I want to learn Japanese, so I'd like to enter this school.

SCHOOL ADMINISTRATOR: *De wa kono gansho ni **kinyū-shite**, nyūgaku o **shinsei-shite** kudasai.*
Then please fill in this application form and apply for admittance.

STUDENT: *Gakuryoku o **kensa-shinai** no desu ka?*
Won't you test my academic ability?

SCHOOL ADMINISTRATOR: *Nichiyōbi ni **shiken-shimasu** node.*
We'll give you a test on Sunday.

STUDENT: *Hiyō wa kakarimasu ka?*
Is there a fee?

SCHOOL ADMINISTRATOR: *Juken ryō go sen en o **nōfu-shite** kudasai. **Juken-shinai** to, **nyūgaku-dekimasen**.*
Please pay five thousand yen for the examination fees. If you do not take the test, you won't be admitted.

STUDENT: *Shiken wa nani go de suru no desu ka?*
What language is the test in?

SCHOOL ADMINISTRATOR: *Eigo ka Chūgokugo de **kaitō-dekimasu**.*
You can answer either in English or in Chinese.

STUDENT: *Shiken wa nanji ni **kaishi-shite**, to nanji ni **shūryō-shimasu** ka?*
What time does the test begin and what time does it finish?

SCHOOL ADMINISTRATOR: *Kuwashii koto wa ano kokuban ni **happyō-shite** arimasu.*
Details are announced on that blackboard over there.

STUDENT: *Sō desu ka. Shiken no kekka wa **tsūchi-shite**
kureru no desu ka?
I see. Do you notify us of the examination results?

SCHOOL ADMINISTRATOR: *Isshū kan inai ni yūbin de **renraku-
shimasu**.*
We'll inform you of the result within a week by
mail.

STUDENT: *Donna kyōkasho o **shiyō-suru** no deshō ka?*
What kind of textbook shall we use?

SCHOOL ADMINISTRATOR: *Shiken no kekka ni yotte gakusei o
kumiwake-shimasu. Kyōkasho wa kumi ni yotte
sōi-shimasu.*
According to the result of the examination, we'll
classify the students into groups. The textbooks
vary from one class to another.

STUDENT: *Shiken ni **gōkaku-sureba**, itsu kara **tōkō-suru**
koto ni narimasu ka?*
If I pass the exam, when do I start coming to school?

SCHOOL ADMINISTRATOR: *Raigetsu no tsuitachi kara **tōkō-
shimasu**. Gozenchū ni nyūgakushiki o **kaisai-shi-
masu** node, zehi **sanka-shite** kudasai. Mae no hi ni
nyūgaku tetsuzuki o **kanryō-shite** kudasai.*
You are to come to school from the first of next

month. In the morning, we will hold an entrance ceremony so please be sure to attend. You must complete the procedures for your enrollment by the previous day.

STRUCTURES AND SYNONYMS

benkyō-suru 勉強する *benkyō* (study, lesson) + *suru*
• to study, to learn
    Compare with *manabu* 学ぶ to study; *keiko-suru* 稽古する to do one's lesson
    *Kanojo wa daigaku de Nihon bungaku o **manande imasu**.*
    She is studying Japanese literature at college.

nyūgaku-suru 入学する *nyūgaku* (enrollment in school) + *suru*
• to enter school, to be admitted to school
    Compare with *gakkō/daigaku ni hairu* 学校/大学に入る to enter school/university
    *Ani wa sakunen Tōdai ni **hairimashita**.*
    My older brother entered Tokyo University last year.

kinyū-suru 記入する *kinyū* (jot down, write, fill in) + *suru*
• to jot down, to write, to fill in
    Compare with *kaku* 書く to write; *kakiireru* 書き入れる to fill in

*Namae wa doko ni **kaku** no desu ka?*
Where should I write my name?

shinsei-suru 申請する *shinsei* (application) + *suru*
• to apply for
  Compare with *negaideru* 願い出る to apply for
  *Murabitotachi wa damu kōji no haishi o **negaideta**.*
  The villagers applied for the cancellation of the dam
  construction.

shiken-suru 試験する *shiken* (test, examination) + *suru*
• to test, to examine, to give an examination
  Compare with *tamesu* 試す to test, to examine
  *Shachō wa watashi no gakuryoku o **tamesu** tame ni
  Eigo de tegami o kakaseta.*
  In order to examine my academic abilities, the presi-
  dent made me write a letter in English.

nōfu-suru 納付する *nōfu* (payment) + *suru*
• to pay
  Compare with *harau* 払う to pay
  *Kare wa gokagetsu bun no gessha o **haratte** imasen.*
  He hasn't payed tuition for five months.

juken-suru 受験する *juken* (test, exam) + *suru*
• to take a test, to take an exam
  Compare with *shiken o ukeru* 試験を受ける to take a
  test
  *Kare wa rainen Waseda o **ukemasu**.*

Next year he'll take the entrance examination for Waseda University.

kaitō-suru 回答する *kaitō* (answer, solution) + *suru*
- to answer, to solve
  Compare with *kotaeru* 答える to answer, to respond, to solve
  *Kanojo wa saigo no shitsumon ni **kotaeraremasen deshita.***
  She was not able to answer the last question.

kaishi-suru 開始する *kaishi* (start, beginning) + *suru*
- to start, to begin
  Compare with *hajimeru* 始める to begin
  *Chichi wa roku ji ni shigoto o **hajimemasu**.*
  Dad starts work at six o'clock.

shūryō-suru 終了する *shūryō* (conclusion, end) + *suru*
- to conclude, to end, to finish
  Compare with *owaru* 終わる to complete, to end, to finish
  *Shiken wa san-ji ni **owatta**.*
  The test ended at three.

happyō-suru 発表する *happyō* (announcement, statement) + *suru*
- to announce, to state, to publicize
  Compare with *kōhyō-suru* 公表する to publicize, to announce

Keisatsu wa shōnen san nin o taihoshita to nobeta ga namae wa kōhyō-shinakatta.
The police said that they arrested three boys but didn't announce their names.

tsūchi-suru 通知する *tsūchi* (notification) + *suru*
• to communicate, to inform, to notify
Compare with *shiraseru* 知らせる to tell, to let know
Kare wa haha ni denpō de nyūshi gōkaku o shiraseta.
He notifed his mother by telegram about his success in the entrance exam.

renraku-suru 連絡する *renraku* (contact, communication) + *suru*
• to contact, to communicate, to get in touch
Compare with *tsūchi-suru* 通知する to communicate, to notify
Shiken no kekka wa raishū tsūchi-shimasu.
We will notify you of the result of the examination next week.

shiyō-suru 使用する *shiyō* (utilization, use) + *suru*
• to utilize, to use, to make use of
Compare with *tsukau* 使う to use
Kanojo wa denwa o tsukatte shōbai o shite iru.
She uses the phone to do business.

kumiwake-suru 組分けする *kumiwake* (division into classes) + *suru*

• to divide into classes

Compare with *kumi ni wakeru* 組に分ける to divide into classes.

*Ichinensei wa san kumi ni **wakeraremashita**.*

The first year students have been divided into three classes.

sōi-suru 相違する *sōi* (difference, deviation) + *suru*
• to differ, to disagree

Compare with *kotonaru* 異なる to differ, to vary

*Kuni ni yori shūkan wa **kotonarimasu**.*

Customs vary from one country to another.

gōkaku-suru 合格する *gōkaku* (success in an exam) + *suru*
• to pass a test, to be successful in an exam

Compare with *ukaru* 受かる to pass an exam

*Kare wa Keiō ni **ukaranakatta**.*

He did not pass the entrance examination for Keio University.

tōkō-suru 登校する *tōkō* (school attendance) + *suru*
• to go to school, to attend school

Compare with *raikō-suru* 来校する to come to school, to visit school

*Asu kyōiku chō ga **raikō-shimasu**.*

Tomorrow the superintendent will visit our school.

kaisai-suru 開催する *kaisai* (opening) + *suru*

• to hold, to open
> Compare with *hiraku* 開く to hold, to give
> *Nichiyōbi ni uchi de pātii o **hirakimasu**.*
> On Sunday we're giving a party at our house.

sanka-suru 参加する *sanka* (attendance, participation) +
suru
• to attend, to take part in, to participate in
> Compare with *deru* 出る to attend
> *Sakuya kekkonshiki ni **demashita**.*
> Last night I attended a wedding ceremony.

kanryō-suru 完了する *kanryō* (completion, conclusion)
+ *suru*
• to complete, to conclude
> Compare with *oeru* 終える to complete, to finish
> *Mokuyōbi made ni shiharai o **oete** kudasai.*
> Please complete your payment by Thursday.

FOR FURTHER STUDY

anki-suru 暗記する *anki* (rote memorization) + *suru*
• to memorize, to learn by heart
> *Shiken no tame kanojo wa sanbyaku no Eigo no
> tango o **anki-shinakereba** naranai.*
> She has to memorize three hundred English words
> for her examination.

yoshū-suru 予習する *yoshū* (preparatory study) + *suru*
• to study in preparation
> *Kanojo wa mainichi ni jikan **yoshū-shimasu**.*
> She studies two hours everyday in preparation for class.

taigaku-suru 退学する *taigaku* (dismissal, withdrawal from school) + *suru*
• to be dismissed from school, to leave school
> *Amari jugyō o saboru to, **taigaku-shinakereba** naranaku narimasu yo.*
> If you skip too many classes, you will have to leave school.

sotsugyō-suru 卒業する *sotsugyō* (graduation) + *suru*
• to graduate
> *Watashi wa go nen mae ni daigaku o **sotsugyō-shimashita**.*
> I graduated from college five years ago.

5

Getting a Job

THE SITUATION

Japan used to be a poor country. Now, it is attracting many foreign workers due to a shortage of manual labor and the high wages offered. What a change!

Are you looking for a job? You may already have a resume, but according to our standard practices, you need to *sakusei-suru* (prepare) your personal history on a pre-printed form, which you can get at any stationery shop. You *kinyū-suru* (fill in) the form with your own data: your academic and vocational career, plus personal information, such as hobbies, health, and marital status. If it's a small company other than a language school, it is imperative for you to *shiyō-suru* (use) Japanese. English will probably not be understood.

The next step is to look at classified ads in the newspapers. Upon finding a suitable job, *denwa-suru* (phone) the company for further information. If it looks good, *yūsō-suru* (mail) in your personal history. They will *tsūchi-suru* (inform) you of the date and time you are to *mensetsu-suru* (interview) with the personnel manager.

Be sure to *tōchaku-suru* (arrive) early. Within a few minutes, a personnel manager will come in and *akushu-suru* (shake hands) with you. *Jikoshōkai-suru* (introduce yourself). The interviewer will begin to *shitsumon-suru* (ask questions) about your past career. He or she may *memo-suru* (take notes) in a notebook. Sometimes companies *shiken-suru* (test) possible employees, as well. Whatever the situation, remember to *bishō-suru* (smile) all the time and *hentō-suru* (respond) clearly. Soon the interview or test will *shūryō-suru* (finish). *Eshaku-suru* (bow) and give the obligatory *yoroshiku onegai shimasu*.

If you are able to *gōkaku-suru* (be successful) in the interview or test, *shussha-suru* (visit the company). Soon you will *tsūkin-suru* (commute) to work by train like all good employees who are lucky enough to *kinmu-suru* (be engaged in work) in a large Japanese city.

No doubt you will often be expected to *zangyō-suru* (work overtime), *settai-suru* (entertain) your important clients at night, and *kitaku-suru* (come home) late. Sooner or later your management will *hyōka-suru* (evaluate) all your hard work; the result being that you *shōkyū-suru* (get a raise) and *shōkaku-suru* (get promoted) in exchange for practically abandoning your family. Naturally your income will *zōka-suru* (increase) while your private time will *genshō-suru* (decrease). You might think you *jikkan-suru* (feel honestly) happy. You will probably even *kakushin-suru* (be convinced) that you are an important person and *shozoku-suru* (belong to) high society now.

Many people *jiman-suru* (boast) about their high position and *bakani-suru* (look down on) people less fortunate, but look out. You may suddenly *sottō-suru* (fall unconscious) due to a stroke while playing golf with your clients.

Wake up people, before you *karōshi-suru* (die of overwork)!

DIALOGUE

MARY: *Moshi, moshi. Jinjika desu ka? Kochira wa Merii Jakuson to mōshimasu. Hara buchō wa **zaisha-shite imasu** ka?*

Hello, is this the personnel section? This is Mary Jackson. Is Mr. Hara in the office?

PERSONNEL OFFICE: *Hai, jinjibu de gozaimasu. Hara wa tadaima **gaishutsu-shite/shutcho-shite orimasu ga**.*

Yes, this is the personnel department. Mr. Hara is out of the office/on a business trip at the moment.

MARY: *Itsu goro **kisha-saremasu** ka?*

When will he be back in the office?

PERSONNEL OFFICE: *Hara wa tōka ni **kisha-shimasu/kikoku-shimasu***.

Mr. Hara will return to the office/return home on the tenth.

MARY: *Jitsu wa ni shūkan mae ni rirekisho o **sōfu-itashi-mashita** ga **tōchaku-shite imasu** deshō ka? Sore o **kakunin-suru** no wa kochira de yoroshii deshō ka?*

To tell the truth, I sent you a personal history two weeks ago. Has it arrived? Is this the right place to confirm such?

PERSONNEL OFFICE: *Hai. Merii Jakuson-san desu ne. Tashika ni **juryō-shite orimasu***.

Yes. Mary Jackson, is it? We have, in fact, received it.

MARY: *Hara buchō wa sore o goran ni natta deshō ka?*

I was wondering if Mr. Hara had a chance to look at it?

PERSONNEL OFFICE: *Hai. **Haiken-shimashita.** Jūgo nichi, ku-ji ni **raisha-shite** kudasai. Sono toki buchō ga anata ni **mensetsu-itashimasu**. Zettai ni **chikoku-shinaide** kudasai.*

Yes, he did. Please come to our company at nine o'clock on the fifteenth. You will be interviewed by our manager at that time. Please don't be late.

MARY: *Wakarimashita. Yoroshiku onegai shimasu. Dōmo arigatō gozaimashita.*
I understand. Thank you very much.

On the day of the interview:

MARY: *Ohayō gozaimasu. Mensetsu kaijō wa doko deshō ka?*
Good morning. Where is the interview room?

RECEPTIONIST: *Hai, go annai-itashimasu. Koko de taiki-shite kudasai. Anata no namae ga anaunsu-saretara, nyūshitsu-shite kudasai. Nokku-suru hitsuyō wa arimasen.*
Yes, I'll take you there. Please wait here. When your name is announced, please enter the room. You don't need to knock.

INTERVIEWER: *Merii Jakuson-san. Dōzo ohairi kudasai.*
Ms. Mary Jackson. Please come in.

MARY: *Ohayō gozaimasu. Merii Jakuson desu. Zehi nyūsha-shitai node yoroshiku onegai itashimasu.*
Good morning. I'm Mary Jackson. By all means, I'd like to enter the company. Thank you for your consideration. (Lit., Please be kind to me.)

INTERVIEWER: *Ima made donna shigoto o keiken-shima-shita ka, setsumei-shite kudasai.*

Please explain what kinds of jobs you've had experience in until now.

MARY: *Eigo o oshieru koto to keiri o **keiken-shimashita***.
I'm experienced in teaching English and accounting.

INTERVIEWER: *Wāpuro wa **sōsa-dekimasu** ka?*
Can you operate a word processor?

MARY: *Hai. Eibun no wāpuro wa dekimasu.*
Yes. I can operate an English word processor.

INTERVIEWER: ***Zangyō-suru** koto ga dekimasu ka?*
Can you work overtime?

MARY: *Nihon no kaisha desu kara, Nihonjin to onaji yō ni **zangyō-suru** tsumori desu.*
It's a Japanese company, so I intend to do overtime just as the Japanese do.

After many questions, the interview is brought to an end.

INTERVIEWER: *Wakarimashita. Mensetsu no kekka wa isshūkan inai ni oshirase itashimasu. Gokurōsama deshita.*
I understand. We will let you know the result of this interview within a week. Thank you for your time.

STRUCTURES AND SYNONYMS

zaiseki-suru 在席する *zaiseki* (to be at one's own desk) + *suru*
- to be at one's seat, to be in the office
  Compare with *iru* いる to be present, to exist
  *Haha wa ima **imasen**.*
  My mother is not in now.

gaishutsu-suru 外出する *gaishutsu* (go out) + *suru*
- to go out
  Compare with *soto e deru* 外へ出る to go out
  *Kanojo wa amari **soto e denai**.*
  She rarely goes out.

shutcho-suru 出張する *shutcho* (business trip) + *suru*
- to travel on business, to go on a business trip

kisha-suru 帰社する *kisha* (return to one's company) + *suru*
- to return to one's company
  Compare with *modoru* 戻る to return
  *Shachō wa go-ji ni **modorimasu**.*
  Our president will return at five.

kikoku-suru 帰国する *kikoku* (return to one's country) + *suru*
- to return to one's country
  Compare with *modoru* 戻る to return

*Kachō wa tōbun **modorimasen**.*
Our manager will not return for a while.

sōfu-suru 送付する *sōfu* (sending, forwarding) + *suru*
• to send, to forward
    Compare with *okuru* 送る to send, to forward
    *Oji ga omoshiroi hon o **okutte** kureta.*
    My uncle sent me an interesting book.

tōchaku-suru 到着する *tōchaku* (arrival) + *suru*
• to arrive, to reach
    Compare with *tsuku* 着く to arrive, to reach
    *Kono densha wa Osaka ni nanji ni **tsukimasu** ka?*
    What time does this train arrive at Osaka?

juryū-suru 受領する *juryō* (receipt) + *suru*
• to receive, to get
    Compare with *uketoru* 受け取る to receive
    *Kinō **uketorimashita**.*
    I received it yesterday.

raisha-suru 来社する *raisha* (coming to a company) + *suru*
• to come to a company, to pay a visit to a company
    Compare with *kaisha ni kuru* 会社に来る to come to a company
    *Asu mata **kaisha ni koraremasu** ka?*
    Can you come to the company again tomorrow?

mensetsu-suru 面接する *mensetsu* (meeting, interview) + *suru*
- to have an interview
    Compare with *au* 会う to see, to meet with
    Kyō jū nin no gakusei ni aimasu.
    Today I will see ten students.

chikoku-suru 遅刻する *chikoku* (lateness) + *suru*
- to be late
    Compare with *okureru* 遅れる to be late
    Densha ni okuretara, takushii de ikimasu.
    If I am late for the train, I'll go by taxi.

anaunsu-suru アナウンスする *anaunsu* (announcement) + *suru*
- to announce, i.e., via a loudspeaker
    Compare with *yobu* 呼ぶ to call
    Namae ga yobaretara, te o agete kudasai.
    When your name is called, please raise your hand.

nyūshitsu-suru 入室する *nyūshitsu* (enter a room) + *suru*
- to enter a room
    Compare with *heya ni hairu* 部屋に入る to enter a
    room
    Kanojo wa heya ni haitte sugu doa o rokku-shita.
    She locked the door as soon as she entered the room.

nokku-suru ノックする *nokku* (knock) + *suru*
- to knock

Compare with *tataku* 叩く to knock
*Gichō wa san kai tēburu o **tataita**.*
The chairman knocked on the table three times.

nyūsha-suru 入社する *nyūsha* (enter a company) + *suru*
• to enter a company
Compare with *kaisha ni hairu* 会社に入る to enter a company
*Itsu **kaisha ni hairimashita** ka?*
When did you join our company?

keiken-suru 経験する *keiken* (experience) + *suru*
• to experience, to be experienced in

setsumei-suru 説明する *setsumei* (explanation) + *suru*
• to explain

sōsa-suru 操作する *sōsa* (run, operate) + *suru*
• to run, to operate, to move
Compare with *ugokasu* 動かす to operate, to move
*Kono kikai wa senmonka shika **ugokasemasen**.*
Only specialists can run this machine.

zangyō-suru 残業する *zangyō* (overtime) + *suru*
• to work overtime

FOR FURTHER STUDY

shozoku-suru 所属する *shozoku* (belong, pertain) + *suru*

• to belong, to pertain
   *Kanojo wa sendenbu ni **shozoku-shite imasu***.
   She belongs to the advertising department.

tainin-suru 退任する *tainin* (resign from a post) + *suru*
• to resign from a post
   *Chichi wa byōki no tame saikin shachō o **tainin-shimashita***.
   Due to illness, my father recently resigned from the presidential post.

shussha-suru 出社する *shussha* (come to one's company, office) + *suru*
• to come to one's company/office, to be present in the office
   *Watashi no chichi wa shibashiba nichiyōbi ni mo **shussha-shimasu***.
   My father often goes to his company even on Sundays.

taishoku-suru 退職する *taishoku* (retirement) + *suru*
• to retire, to quit
   *Kare wa sakunen **taishoku-shite**, ima daigaku de benkyō-shite iru.*
   He retired last year and now studies at college.

6

Doing Business

THE SITUATION

Whether you *shozoku-suru* (belong to) a foreign or Japanese company, the object of your business activities is the same: to *tsuikyū-suru* (pursue) profits. In order to *kakutoku-suru* (obtain) these profits, you must *hanbai-suru* (sell) products that have a high profit margin. In order to *seikō-suru* (succeed) in your sales, it's necessary to *seizō-suru* (manufacture) goods and offer low-priced products. It's also important to *senden-suru* (advertise) your products.

In addition to these basics, you have your essential daily sales activities. For example, you must *hōmon-suru* (visit) your clients' offices and shops. It's very important for a businessperson to give clients a good impression. You *bishō-suru* (smile) and *ojigi-suru* (bow your head) deeply at the reception desk. The receptionist will introduce you to a company representative. You *kōkan-suru* (exchange) your name cards. Now you can *setsumei-suru* (explain) your merchandise. *Kyōchō-suru* (stress) the advantageous features of your products and *teikyō-suru* (offer) your best price. The other party will surely *yōkyū-suru* (request) a lower price. Your opponent might even *kyohi-suru* (refuse) your price. It's time to *kōshō-suru* (negotiate) with your clients over sales conditions. Very often you may find you have to *dakyō-suru* (compromise). But it's also important to know when to stand your ground and *shuchō-suru* (insist) on your position. If you *seikō-suru* (succeed), the company will go ahead and *hatchū-suru* (place an order).

When you *juchū-suru* (receive an order), make sure you have an order confirmation sheet and that your new partner in business will *shōmei-suru* (sign) it. Having wrapped everything up, you can *shiji-suru* (instruct) your factory about the destination, time of dispatch, packing, and so on.

Another obligation of this type of business is to *sanka-suru* (take part in) product shows. Here you can *shutten-suru* (demonstrate) your product's merits. At the show, many companies will *haifu-suru* (distribute) leaflets and catalogues to the visitors. These pamphlets explain how to *jitsuen-suru* (operate) the various products.

Each month you must *keisan-suru* (calculate) your sales totals and *teishutsu-suru* (submit) a report to your boss. If sales *geraku-suru* (go down) or *genshō-suru* (decrease), your boss will *shitta-suru* (scold) you. When your sales *jōshō-suru* (go up), your boss will still *gekirei-suru* (encourage) you to sell even more and *settei-suru* (set) an even higher sales target. Now you'll have to *doryoku-suru* (exert yourself) to *tassei-suru* (achieve) the newly set goal. That's how it goes in the business world.

In a typical sales meeting your boss will *happyō-suru* (announce) his sales policy for the employees to *tōron-suru* (discuss). You may *hantai-suru* (oppose) the plan. But once you *kōryo-suru* (consider) the negative ramifications of opposing your boss, you too will no doubt be obliged to *sansei-suru* (agree) to the plan.

DIALOGUE

SUPERVISOR: *Yamada-san, go-ji ni zenin kaigishitsu ni* **shūgō-sasete** *kudasai. Shinseihin o* **happyō-shimasu** *node.*

Mr. Yamada, please have all employees gather in the meeting room at five. I'll be announcing a new product.

YAMADA: *Wakarimashita. Sono shinseihin o* **haiken-shitai** *no desu ga. Jitsu wa, go-ji made ni* **benkyō-shite** *okitai to omoimasu. Shucho ga chokusetsu* **setsumei-saremasu** *ka?*

Very well. I'd like to see the product. Actually, I think I'd like to study it before five o'clock. Would you explain it yourself directly?

SUPERVISOR: *Ano todana ni **hokan-shite** arimasu. Shiyō setsumeisho o **sanshō-shite**, **chōsa-shite** mite kudasai. Kinō **tōchaku-shita** bakari de, watashi mo mada yoku **kenkyū-shite** imasen.*
It's kept in that shelf. Refer to the operating manual and see if it works. It just arrived yesterday, so I haven't examined it yet either.

Yamada examines the new product.

YAMADA: *Kore ni **sōtō-suru** Nihon seihin wa kanari yasuku **hanbai-sarete orimasu**. Kinō mo yori ōi node, Nihon shijō de **kyōsō-suru** koto wa taihen konnan desu. Dono kurai ni kakaku o **settei-suru** no desu ka?*
Japanese products which correspond to this are sold quite cheaply and have more features. It's pretty difficult to compete with them in the Japanese market. About how much is the price set at?

SUPERVISOR: *Mazu Nihon seihin no seinō to kakaku o yoku **chōsa-shite**, **hikaku-shite** miru hitsuyō ga arimasu. Kouriten to mo **sōdan-shimashō**.*
First of all, we have to investigate the features and prices of Japanese products and compare them with ours. Let's consult with retailers as well.

YAMADA: *Mikka made ni hanbai kachō ni hikaku hyō o **sakusei-sase**, yokka ni kaigi o **kaisai-shite**, kakaku o **kettei-shimashō**.*

I'll have the sales manager make the comparison
table by the third, and on the fourth we'll hold a
meeting and decide the price.

SUPERVISOR: *Sore kara kono seihin no kakaku to seinō o*
kōryo-shinagara, *hanbai keikaku o* **sakusei-shite**
tōka made ni **teishutsu-shite** *kudasai.*
Also please prepare a sales plan for this product,
considering the price and features, and submit it to
me by the tenth.

YAMADA: *Terebi de* **senden-shi,** *mata kouriten o* **shōtai-
suru** *yō ni sendenbu ni* **junbi-sasemasu.** *Demo yō ni
gojū dai* **hassō-suru** *yō ni honsha ni* **yōkyu-shite**
itadakemasu ka?
I'll have the ad department prepare something to
advertise on TV and also to invite retailers. Can you
request the head office to dispatch fifty sets for a
demonstration?

SUPERVISOR: *Hai. Yatte mimashō. Gokurōsan desu,
Yamada-san.*
Yes. I'll see what I can do. Mr. Yamada, Good
work.

STRUCTURES AND SYNONYMS

shūgō-suru 集合する *shūgō* (gather) + *suru*
• to gather, to get together

Compare with *atsumaru* 集まる to gather, to get together

*Kokoni go-ji ni **atsumatte** kudasai.*

Please gather here at five.

happyō-suru 発表する *happyō* (announcement, publication) + *suru*

• to announce, to publicize

Compare with *kōhyō-suru* 公表する to announce, to publicize

*Miseinensha no namae wa **kōhyō-saremasen deshita**.*

The minor's name was not announced.

hokan-suru 保管する *hokan* (keep, store) + *suru*

• to keep, to store

Compare with *shimatte oku* しまっておく to keep, to store

*Ano shorui o kinko ni **shimaimashita** ka?*

Have you kept that document in the safe?

sanshō-suru 参照する *sanshō* (reference, consultation) + *suru*

• to refer to, to consult

Compare with *miru* 見る to see, to refer

*Kanojo wa jisho o **minai** to tegami ga kakenai.*

She can't write a letter without referring to a dictionary.

kenkyū-suru 研究する *kenkyū* (study, research, investigation) + *suru*
• to study, to research, to investigate
   Compare with *shiraberu* 調べる to study, to research, to investigate
   *Shiyō-sarete iru buhin o **shirabemashita**.*
   I checked the parts used in it.

sōtō-suru 相当する *sōtō* (correspondence, proportion) + *suru*
• to correspond, to match, to be proportionate
   Compare with *atehamaru* 当てはまる to correspond, to match, to be proportionate
   *Kare wa shūnyū ni **atehamaranai** gōkana seikatsu o shite iru.*
   He lives an extravagant life which does not match his income.

hanbai-suru 販売する *hanbai* (sale, marketing) + *suru*
• to sell, to market
   Compare with *uru* 売る to sell, to market
   *Sērusuman wa tsuki ni jū dai no kuruma o **uranakereba naranai**.*
   The salesman must sell ten cars a month.

kyōsō-suru 競争する *kyōsō* (competition, race) + *suru*
• to compete, to contest, to race
   Compare with *kisou* 競う to compete, to contend

*Senmu wa shachō to kenryoku o **kisotte iru***.
The executive director competes with the president
for power.

settei-suru 設定する *settei* (setting) + *suru*
• to fix, to establish, to set
   Compare with *sadameru* 定める to fix, to establish,
   to set
   *Seifu wa atarashii zeiritsu o **sadameta***.
   The government set new tax rates.

chōsa-suru 調査する *chōsa* (research, survey, investigation) + *suru*
• to survey, to investigate
   Compare with *shiraberu* 調べる to survey, to investigate
   *Kare wa kakkoku de no shijō kakaku o **shirabete
   imasu***.
   He is investigating the market prices of each
   country.

hikaku-suru 比較する *hikaku* (comparison) + *suru*
• to compare
   Compare with *kuraberu* 比べる to compare
   *Kono kuruma to ano kuruma o **kurabemashō***.
   Let's compare this car with that one.

sōdan-suru 相談する *sōdan* (consultation) + *suru*
• to consult

Compare with *hanashiau* 話し合う to talk to each other, to discuss
*Kare wa kekkon ni tsuite haha to **hanashiatta**.*
He talked with his mother about his marriage.

sakusei-suru 作成する *sakusei* (preparation, making) + *suru*
• to make, to prepare
Compare with *tsukuru* 作る to make, to prepare
*Asu made ni hanbai keikaku o **tsukutte** kudasai.*
Please prepare a sales plan by tomorrow.

kaisai-suru 開催する *kaisai* (hold, open) + *suru*
• to hold, to open
Compare with *moyoosu* 催す to hold, to open
*Watsusha wa nen ni kai dairiten kaigi o **moyooshite imasu**.*
Our company holds two distribution meetings a year.

kettei-suru 決定する *kettei* (decision) + *suru*
• to decide
Compare with *kimeru* 決める to decide
*Shachō wa seihin no nesage o **kimemashita**.*
The president has decided on the price reduction of our products.

senden-suru 宣伝する *senden* (propaganda, advertisement, publicity) + *suru*
• to propagandize, to advertise, to publicize

Compare with *iihiromeru* 言い広める to promote, to propagate

Kirisuto no oshie wa sekaijū ni iihiromerareta.

Christ's teachings were propagated all over the world.

shōtai-suru 招待する *shōtai* (invitation) + *suru*
* to invite

Compare with *maneku* 招く to invite

Haiyū wa kekkonshiki ni gohyaku nin no kyaku o manekimashita.

The actor invited five hundred guests to his wedding.

hassō-suru 発送する *hassō* (dispatch) + *suru*
* to dispatch, to forward

Compare with *okuridasu* 送り出す to dispatch, to forward

Wareware wa kesa terebi o nisen dai okuridashita.

We dispatched two thousand television sets this morning.

yōkyū-suru 要求する *yōkyū* (request, demand) + *suru*
* to request, to demand

Compare with *motomeru* 求める to request, to demand

Shichō wa kenchiku gaisha ni wairo o motomeru darō.

The mayor will request that the construction company offer him a bribe.

FOR FURTHER STUDY

kaihatsu-suru 開発する *kaihatsu* (development) + *suru*
• to develop
> *Wagasha wa saikin kōseinō konpyūtā o **kaihatsu-shimashita**.*
> Our firm recently developed a high-performance computer.

sōkin-suru 送金する *sōkin* (money remittance) + *suru*
• to remit money
> *Honsha wa wareware ni goman doru **sōkin-suru** yotei desu.*
> The head office is scheduled to remit to us fifty thousand dollars.

nesage-suru 値下げする *nesage* (price cut, reduction) + *suru*
• to cut the price, to lower the price
> *Tasha to kyōsō-suru tame ni, wareware wa **nesage-suru** koto o yoginaku-sareta.*
> In order to compete with our competitors, we were obliged to lower our prices.

neage-suru 値上げする *neage* (price hike) + *suru*
• to hike the price, to raise the price
> *Kosuto daka ni taisho-suru tame, tōsha wa seihin o **neage-suru** koto ni kettei-shita.*
> In order to cope with the high costs, our company decided to raise the price of our products.

7

Traveling

THE SITUATION

Hyakubun wa ikken ni shikazu (Seeing is believing). To know Japan well, you should visit as many places as possible. Whether you want to go on a trip to one of Japan's many sightseeing spots and stay at a famous hotel, or simply enjoy an evening out at a first class restaurant, you've got to first *yoyaku-suru* (make reservations) in advance. To *kanshō-suru* (appreciate) a cultural event, such as a play, or to *ryokō-suru* (travel) by bullet train or on a luxurious cruise ship, you have to *kōnyū-suru* (purchase) a special ticket. So many things to do and so many places to see! Luckily, you can always *irai-suru* (ask) a travel agent for advice. He or she is always ready to *kyōryoku-suru* (cooperate) and *jogen-suru* (advise) clients. After you *kenkyū-suru* (research) the myriad of possible destinations and conditions, make the leap and *sentaku-suru* (choose) one.

The travel agent will *nyūryoku-suru* (input) necessary data into the computer to *chekku-suru* (check) the booking. Once the agent can *kakunin-suru* (confirm) a vacancy or an available ticket, you must *nōnyū-suru* (pay) the fare. Your agent will then *hakkō-suru* (issue) a ticket. In the event your plans change and you wish to *tsuika-suru* (add) two or three persons to your trip, the agent will undoubtedly *kangei-suru* (welcome) it.

On the day of departure, try not to *chikoku-suru* (be late). As soon as you *tōchaku-suru* (reach) the appointed gathering place, *teiji-suru* (show) your ticket to your tour conductors. They will *annai-suru* (guide) you to the platform or to the sightseeing bus. Hurry up and *jōsha-suru* (get on board)! On weekends and holidays trains can often *konzatsu-suru* (be crowded) with many people. So please *chakuseki-suru* (sit down) quickly in your reserved seat. If you are on the train, you'll be able to hear the loudspeaker *hōsō-suru* (announce) its destinations and arrival times together with other notices and warnings. On a bus, a friendly guide will *kangei-suru* (welcome) you on board and *setsumei-suru* (explain) all about your trip. The bus driver will *unten-suru* (drive) while the guide's duty is to *sewa-suru* (take care of) the passengers. As you relax and listen, your train or bus will *hassha-suru* (start) for your destination.

Often, a tour bus will *teisha-suru* (stop) to *kyūkei-suru* (take a short break). Go ahead and get out to *senobi-suru* (stretch), but *chūi-suru* (watch) the time. If you *chikoku-suru* (delay), it will *meiwaku-suru* (annoy, cause inconvenience) to other passengers. A Japanese proverb says, *Tabi no haji wa kakisute* (We are apt to feel free to do shameful things when traveling), but don't be tempted to throw your trash on the ground or to commit other such disgraceful acts.

Arriving at the sightseeing spot or hotel at which you are to *shukuhaku-suru* (stay overnight), the bus will *chūsha-suru* (park). It's time for you to *gesha-suru* (get out of the vehicle). The bus guide will *yūdō-suru* (conduct) you to the right place. Be sure to *kinen satsuei-suru* (take souvenir pictures). After all, you'll want to show them to your friends and family, won't you?

DIALOGUE

MARY: *Sumimasen ga, kinō Nikkō basu ryokō o **yoyaku-shita** no desu ga. Kippu wa toremashita ka?*
Excuse me, I made a reservation for the bus to Nikko yesterday. Did you get our seats?

TRAVEL AGENT: *Sō desu ne. Ima kūseki o **chekku-itashi-masu**. Jūgonichi o-futari sama desu ne.*
Let's see. I'll check the reservation's status now. Two persons on the fifteenth, right?

The agent checks his computer for a moment for the reservation.

TRAVEL AGENT: *Kochira desu. Futaribun no seki o kakuho-shimashita. Ima sugu kippu o hakkō-itashimasu.*
Here it is. The two seats have been secured. I'll issue the tickets right now.

MARY: *Yokatta! Dōmo arigatō.*
Great! Thank you.

The day of Mary and Mayumi's departure arrives.

MAYUMI: *Sumimasen, gaido-san, zen'in shūgō-shimashita ka? Mō shuppatsu-suru jikan desu.*
Excuse me, guide, has everyone gathered? It's already time to leave.

GUIDE: *Shuppatsu jikan wa keika-shimashita ga, mada ato sannin tōchaku-shite imasen node, shuppatsu-dekimasen. Mō sukoshi, shinbō-shite itadakemasen ka?*
It is past our departure time, but three people haven't arrived yet, so we can't leave. If you could please have a little more patience . . .

MAYUMI: *Hora, tōchaku-shimashita. Sā shuppatsu-shimashō.*
Here they come. All right, let's leave.

GUIDE: *Minasan, ohayō gozaimasu. Honjitsu wa tōsha no basu o go-riyō itadaki makotoni arigatō gozaimasu.*

*San-ji no tōchaku o **yotei-shite** orimasu ga, dōro ga **jūtai-shite imasu** node, ni-jikan gurai no okure wa **kakugo-shinakereba naranai** deshō.*

Good morning, everyone. Thank you very much for using our bus today. We're scheduled to arrive at three, but as the road is crowded we must be prepared for a delay of roughly two hours.

The bus finally arrives at their destination.

GUIDE: *Hai, koko de **gesha-shite**, Tōshōgū o **kanran-shimasu**. Kono kippu de zenbu **nyūjō-dekimasu**. Koko ni **chūsha-shimasu** node, yo-ji made ni **jōsha-shite** kudasai. Dare ka shitsumon wa arimasu ka?*

OK. We'll get off here and see Tōshōgū Shrine. You can enter any of the sights with this ticket. We'll park here, please be back on by four. Does anyone have any questions?

MARY: *Omiyage o kaitai no desu ga.*

I'd like to buy souvenirs.

GUIDE: *Ato de omiyageya ni annai-itashimasu. **Kaimono-shitai** kata wa sono toki ni dōzo. Otsukare no kata wa kuruma de **kyūkei-shite** ite mo kekkō desu. Yōmei-mon no mae de kinen shashin o **satsuei-shimasu** node dekirudake **sanka-shite** kudasai.*

Later we'll take you to souvenir shops. Those who want to shop, please do so at that time. If you're tired, you can take a rest in the bus. We'll be taking a group photo in front of Yōmei Gate. Please join us if you can.

STRUCTURES AND SYNONYMS

hakkō-suru 発行する *hakkō* (issuance) + *suru*
- to issue
    Compare with *sakusei-suru* 作成する to prepare, to make
    Taishikan de atarashii pasupōto o sakusei-shite moraimashita.
    I had a new passport made by the embassy.

kakuho-suru 確保する *kakuho* (security, assurance) + *suru*
- to secure, assure, guarantee
    Compare with *te ni ireru* 手に入れる to secure, to acquire, to have in hand
    Ensōkai no kippu o ni mai te ni ireta.
    I got two tickets for the concert.

shūgō-suru 集合する *shūgō* (assembly, gathering) + *suru*
- to assemble, to gather
    Compare with *atsumaru* 集まる to assemble, to gather, to get together
    Sakuya no ōkii pātii ni nannin atsumarimashita ka?
    How many people gathered for last night's big party?

shuppatsu-suru 出発する *shuppatsu* (departure, start) + *suru*

• to depart, to leave, to start
   Compare with *deru* 出る to depart, to leave
   *Chichi wa Pari o nichiyōbi ni **deta**.*
   My father left Paris on Sunday.

keika-suru 経過する *keika* (lapse) + *suru*

• to elapse, to pass, to run
   Compare with *sugiru* 過ぎる to pass
   *Are kara go nen **sugita**.*
   Five years have passed since then.

tōchaku-suru 到着する *tōchaku* (arrival) + *suru*

• to arrive, to reach
   Compare with *tsuku* 着く to arrive, to reach
   *Tōkyō ni **tsuitara** denwa o kudasai.*
   On arriving at Tokyo, please give me a phone call.

shinbō-suru 辛抱する *shinbō* (endurance, patience) + *suru*

• to endure, to be patient, to forbear
   Compare with *taeru* 耐える to endure, to stand, to bear
   *Kanojo wa fukutsū ni hito-ban **taenakereba** nara-nakatta.*
   She had to endure a stomachache all through the night.

yotei-suru 予定する *yotei* (schedule, expectation) + *suru*
• to be scheduled, to expect, to plan
> Compare with *tsumori de aru* 積もりである to intend, to plan
> *Osaka ni mikka taizai-suru **tsumoridatta**.*
> I intended to stay in Osaka for three days.

jūtai-suru 渋滞する *jūtai* (delay) + *suru*
• to be delayed, to be jammed
> Compare with *komu* 込む to be crowded, to be conjested
> *Dōro ga konde ita node **okureta**.*
> We were late because of the traffic jam.

kakugo-suru 覚悟する *kakugo* (readiness, preparation) + *suru*
• to be ready, to be prepared
> Compare with *kokoroeru* 心得る to understand, to be aware of
> *Hito wa shinu mono to **kokoroenasai**.*
> Be aware that man is mortal.

gesha-suru 下車する *gesha* (get out, disembark) + *suru*
• to get off or out of a vehicle, to disembark
> Compare with *oriru* 降りる to get off, to get out, to alight
> *Kanojo wa Shinbashi de densha o **orita**.*
> She got off the train at Shinbashi.

kanran-suru 観覧する (view, watch) + *suru*
- to view, to watch, to see
  Compare with *miru* 見る to see, to view
  *Daibutsu o **mita** ato chūshoku o torimasu.*
  After viewing the statue of Buddha, we will have lunch.

nyūjō-suru 入場する *nyūjō* (entrance, admission) + *suru*
- to enter, to be admitted to
  Compare with *hairu* 入る to enter, to get in
  *Eigakan ni roku-ji ni **hairimashō**.*
  Let's enter the movie theater at six.

chūsha-suru 駐車する *chūsha* (park) + *suru*
- to park
  Compare with *tomeru* 止める to park (literally, "to stop")
  *Kare wa maiban dōro ni kuruma o **tomete iru**.*
  He parks his car on the road every night.

jōsha-suru 乗車する *jōsha* (get on or into a vehicle) + *suru*
- to get on or in a vehicle, to take a bus/train
  Compare with *noru* 乗る to ride, to take a bus/train
  *Maiasa basu ni **noranaide** eki made arukimasu.*
  I walk to the station every morning; I don't take the bus.

kaimono-suru 買い物する *kaimono* (shopping, purchase) + *suru*

- to shop

  Compare with *kau* 買う to buy, to purchase

  Sūpā de kudamono o kaimashita.

  I bought fruit at the supermarket.

kyūkei-suru 休憩する *kyūkei* (rest, break) + *suru*

- to take a rest, to take a break

  Compare with *yasumu* 休む to rest, to have a break, to take a holiday

  Kokode sukoshi yasumimashō.

  Let's take a little rest here.

satsuei-suru 撮影する *satsuei* (photograph) + *suru*

- to take a picture, to photograph

  Compare with *shashin o toru* 写真を取る to photograph, to take a picture

  Fujisan no shashin o san mai torimashita.

  I took three pictures of Mt. Fuji.

sanka-suru 参加する *sanka* (participation, attendance) + *suru*

- to join, to take part in

  Compare with *deru* 出る to join, to attend

  Zannen desu ga shinnenkai ni deraremasen.

  Regrettably, I can't attend the New Year's party.

FOR FURTHER STUDY

maebarai-suru 前払する *maebarai* (pre-payment) + *suru*
• to pay in advance
> *Ryohi wa **maebarai-shite** kudasai.*
> Please pay the travel expenses in advance.

kyanseru machi-suru キャンセル待ちする *kyanseru machi* (wait for a cancellation) + *suru*
• to wait for a cancellation
> *Narita de takusan no hito ga **kyanseru machi**-shite imashita.*
> A lot of people were waiting at Narita for cancellations.

pusshu-suru プッシュする *pusshu* (push) + *suru*
• to push
> *Ryokōsha o mō ichido **pusshu-shimashō**.*
> I'll push the travel agent once more.

dannen-suru 断念する *dannen* (give up, abandon) + *suru*
• to give up, to abandon
> *Hoteru no yoyaku ga dekinakatta node, kare wa ryokō o **dannen-shimashita**.*
> Since he couldn't make hotel reservations, he gave up on his trip.

8

Taking Care of Your Health

THE SITUATION

Regardless of sex, race, or religion, everyone will surely *sansei-suru* (agree) to the following Japanese proverb: *Inochi atte no mono da ne* (Life must be the first consideration). Another wise proverb states, *Kenkō wa tomi ni masaru* (Health is better than wealth). If you are in a foreign country, you must especially *chūi-suru* (take care) of your health. So let's learn the following easy-to-use *suru* verbs which can serve to keep you healthy and may even save your life.

If you *muri-suru* (do something to excess) in anything, you will surely *shōmō-suru* (be exhausted). Exhaustion makes it easy to *kansen-suru* (be infected) with a disease. It's easy for germs to *sennyū-suru* (sneak) into an exhausted body too weak to *teikō-suru* (resist) such an invasion.

If you do become sick, you should go to a hospital. The doctor will *shinsatsu-suru* (examine) you, *shindan-suru* (diagnose), and *chiryō-suru* (treat) you. For example, the doctor may *chūsha-suru* (inject) drugs into your veins. Sometimes you must *tsūin-suru* (go to the hospital regularly) for such treatment.

Occasionally, it is too difficult for a doctor to specifically *shindan-suru* (diagnose) your illness. He may need to *kensa-suru* (examine) you more thoroughly with special medical equipment. He may *satsuei-suru* (take X-rays), *saishu-suru* (take) a blood sample, and *sokutei-suru* (measure, take) your blood pressure. As many kinds of diseases *densen-suru* (spread by contagion), hospitals regularly *shōdoku-suru* (disinfect) all medical equipment used in these procedures.

Let's hope you don't have a serious disease. But if you do, the doctor may need to *shujutsu-suru* (operate) on you. In most cases requiring an operation, you must *nyūin-suru* (be hospitalized) for a few weeks. If the operation should *shippai-suru* (fail), the worst case scenario is to *shibō-suru* (die). But don't worry. Of course the doctor will *seikō-suru* (succeed) in his operation! You will *zenkai-suru* (recover completely) and *taiin-suru* (leave the hospital) in a few days or so. If you had decided instead to *hōchi-suru* (leave your disease to chance), there would have been a greater possibility for it to *akka-suru* (grow worse). For the lucky person, however, time may *chiyu-suru* (heal) it all by itself. Best not to test your luck in these matters though!

Other painful aspects of an illness are the unexpected expenses that will no doubt *hassei-suru* (be incurred). When you *gōkei-suru* (total) overall expenses, you may *hakken-suru* (find) that the costs can quickly *tōtatsu-suru* (reach) an amount you can no longer afford. Some seriously ill patients even *zetsubō-suru* (become desperate) and *jisatsu-suru* (commit suicide) in such a predicament.

What would you do? You must *shakkin-suru* (borrow money) or *yonige-suru* (fly by night). Well, there is a better solution. Get health insurance. Remember: *Korobanu saki no tsue* (Forewarned is forearmed). How about a cheaper way, you ask? The cheapest way of course, is to *sessei-suru* (exercise moderation) in everything, namely eating, drinking, playing, and working.

DIALOGUE

MASAO: *Watashi no tomodachi wa senshū **karōshi-shite** shimaimashita. **Hirō-shite iru** ni mo kakawarazu, maiban **zangyō-shite imashita**.*

A friend of mine died of fatigue from overwork last week. In spite of being tired, he worked overtime every night.

MARY: *Dōshite Nihonjin wa **shibō-suru** made shigoto o keizoku-suru no ka? Naze **kyūyō-shinai** no desu ka?*

Why do the Japanese continue working until they die? Why don't they take a rest?

MASAO: *Moshi kyūka o toru to, jōshi wa anata ga namake-mono to omou kamo shiremasen. Karōshi-shita to-modachi wa jōshi ya buka no mae ni **taisha-suru** no wa burei de aru to itte imashita.*

If you take a holiday, your superiors may think that you are lazy. My friend who died of overwork used to say that it was not polite to leave the office before his bosses and other staff members.

MARY: *Sore dewa jūbun ni yasumu jikan mo nemuru jikan mo nakunarimasu ne.*

No wonder he didn't have enough time to take a rest or even to sleep.

MASAO: *Tokorode, asu chichi ga i no shuyō o **shujutsu-shimasu** node **kanbyō-shinakereba narimasen**. Asu wa **kekkin-shimasu** node yoroshiku.*

By the way my father will be operated on for a tumor in his stomach tomorrow. I've got to look after him so I'll be absent tomorrow.

MARY: *Sore wa komarimashita ne. Itsu **nyūin-shimashita** ka?*

That's too bad. When was he hospitalized?

MASAO: *Mikka mae ni **kensa-shita** kekka, shuyō ga **hakken-saremashita**. Isha wa ima **shujutsu-sureba**, **kanchi-suru** to iimashita.*

He was examined three days ago and as a result, a

tumor was discovered. The doctor says that if he's operated on now, he'll be completely cured.

MARY: *Sōki ni **hakken-shite** yokatta desu ne. Teikiteki ni **kenshin-shite** morau koto ga taisetsu desu. Tonikaku **fusessei-suru** koto ga warui no desu.*
He's lucky it was found early. It's important to have check-ups regularly. At any rate, it's no good being intemperate.

MASAO: *Sono tōri desu. Hokkaidō ni **tanshin funin-shite** kara, sake no ryō ga **zōka-shi**, kecchū koresuterōru no atai ga **jōshō-shita** sō desu.*
That's right. He says that since he went to Hokkaido for his new post without the rest of the family, the amount of alcohol he drank increased and his cholesterol level went up as well.

MARY: *Sore wa tōzen deshō. Kazoku ga inai to sabishii kara ne.*
That's natural. Anyone will be lonely without their family.

MASAO: *Shinzō hossa o **bōshi-suru** tame ni, kare wa kusuri o **fukuyō-suru** koto to, yasai o oku **sesshu-suru** yō ni isha kara **shiji-saremashita**. **Taiin-shitara**, san-kagetsu **kyūyō-seyo** to no meirei desu ga, chichi wa mō shigoto no koto o **shinpai-shite imasu**.*
In order to prevent a heart attack, the doctor in-

structed him to take some medicine and eat a lot of vegetables. In spite of the order to take a rest for three months after leaving the hospital, my father is already worried about his work.

MARY: *Tonikaku shujutsu go wa shigoto no koto wa tōbun wasurete, jūbun ni **ryōyō-suru** yō ni itte kudasai. Sore dewa odaijini!*

Even so, please tell him to forget about work after the operation for a while and to recuperate fully. And take care!

STRUCTURES AND SYNONYMS

karōshi-suru 過労死する *karōshi* (death due to overwork) + *suru*
• to die due to overwork

hirō-suru 疲労する *hirō* (fatigue, tiredness) + *suru*
• to be fatigued, to get tired
   Compare with *tsukareru* 疲れる to be fatigued, to get tired
   ***Tsukaretara**, yasunde kudasai.*
   Please take a rest if you get tired.

shibō-suru 死亡する *shibō* (death) + *suru*
• to die
   Compare with *shinu* 死ぬ to die

*Kare ga **shinu** toki, karera wa nanbyakuman doru
mo sōzoku-suru deshō ne.*
They will inherit millions of dollars when he dies.

keizoku-suru 継続する *keizoku* (continuation) + *suru*
• to continue
  Compare with *tsuzukeru* 続ける to continue
  *Shigoto o **tsuzukemashō**.*
  Let's continue our work.

kyūyō-suru 休養する *kyūyō* (rest, repose) + *suru*
• to take a rest, to repose
  Compare with *yasumu* 休む to take a rest, to repose
  *Chichi wa **yasumanaide** go-jikan mo hataraite iru.*
  My father has been working for five hours without
  taking a rest.

taisha-suru 退社する *taisha* (withdrawal, retirement from
a company) + *suru*
• to leave one's office, to retire from a company
  Compare with *kaisha o deru* 会社を出る to leave
  one's office; *kaisha o yameru* 会社をやめる to retire
  from a company
  *Kyō nanji ni kaisha o **deta** no?*
  What time did you leave your office today?

shujutsu-suru 手術する *shujutsu* (operation) + *suru*
• to undergo an operation, to perform an operation

Compare with *kiru* 切る to cut, to undergo an operation, to perform an operation
*Kare wa gan de hara o nikai **kitta**.*
Due to cancer he had his stomach operated on twice.

kanbyō-suru 看病する *kanbyō* (nurse, attend to) + *suru*
• to nurse, to attend
Compare with *miru* 看る to nurse, to look after, to take care of
*Kanojo wa byōki no haha o ninen kan **mite** kita.*
She has been nursing her sick mother for two years.

kekkin-suru 欠勤する *kekkin* (absence from work) + *suru*
• to be absent from work
Compare with *kaisha o yasumu* 会社を休む to be absent from work
*Kanojo wa **kaisha o yasunde**, Atami de dēto-shita.*
She was absent from work for a date in Atami.

nyūin-suru 入院する *nyūin* (hospitalization) + *suru*
• to be hospitalized
Compare with *hairu* 入る to enter a hospital, to be hospitalized
*Haha wa shiritsu byōin ni mō nikagetsu **haitte imasu**.*
My mother has been hospitalized in the city hospital for two months.

kanchi-suru 完治する *kanchi* (complete recovery) + *suru*
- to recover completely
  Compare with *kanzen ni naoru* 完全に治る to recover completely, to be cured completely
  *Chichi no i wa **kanzen ni naotte imasu**.*
  My father's stomach has been completely cured.

kenshin-suru 検診する *kenshin* (medical examination) + *suru*
- to examine
  Compare with *shiraberu* 調べる to check, to examine
  *Kanojo wa kinō kanzō o **shirabete** moratta.*
  She had her liver examined yesterday.

fusossei-suru 不節制する *fusessei* (intemperance, excess) + *suru*
- to be intemperate, to commit excesses
  Compare with *mucha o suru* 無茶をする to be intemperate
  *Kare wa wakai toki hijō ni **mucha o shita** node, wakajini-shita.*
  Due to extreme intemperance in his youth, he died young.

funin-suru 赴任する *funin* (departure for a new post) + *suru*
- to leave for one's new post

zōka-suru 増加する *zōka* (increase, growth) + *suru*
- to increase, to grow
    Compare with *fueru* 増える to increase, to grow
    *Saikin Nihon no jinkō wa amari **fuemasen**.*
    Lately, Japan's population hasn't increased much.

jōshō-suru 上昇する *jōshō* (rise) + *suru*
- to rise, to go up
    Compare with *agaru* 上がる to rise, to raise
    *Saikin bukka wa sukoshi zutsu **agatte imasu**.*
    Recently the prices of commodities are rising little by little.

bōshi-suru 防止する *bōshi* (prevention, check) + *suru*
- to prevent, to check
    Compare with *fusegu* 防ぐ to prevent, to check
    *Teki no shinnyū o **fusegu** tame takai kabe ga kizukareta.*
    In order to prevent an enemy invasion, high walls were constructed.

fukuyō-suru 服用する *fukuyō* (take medicine) + *suru*
- to take medicine
    Compare with *nomu* 飲む to drink, to take (medicine)
    *Mai shokugo san jō **nominasai**.*
    Take three tablets after every meal.

sesshu-suru 摂取する *sesshu* (intake) + *suru*
- to take in, to ingest
    Compare with *toru* 取る to take, to ingest
    Bitamin C o ōku toreba, kono byōki wa naorimasu.
    If you take a lot of vitamin C, you'll cure this illness.

shiji-suru 指示する *shiji* (instruction, direction) + *suru*
- to instruct, to direct, to order
    Compare with *meirei-suru* 命令する to order, to direct
    Isha wa chichi ni tabako o yameru yō ni meirei-shita.
    The doctor ordered my father to stop smoking.

taiin-suru 退院する *taiin* (departure from a hospital) + *suru*
- to leave a hospital
    Compare with *deru* 出る to go out, to leave
    Haha wa shujutsu go nishūkan de byōin o demashita.
    Two weeks after the operation, my mother left the hospital.

shinpai-suru 心配する *shinpai* (worry) + *suru*
- to worry
    Compare with *anjiru* 案じる to worry
    Kare wa musuko no shōrai o anjite iru.
    He worries about his son's future.

FOR FURTHER STUDY

ninshin-suru 妊娠する *ninshin* (pregnancy, conception) + *suru*
- to become pregnant, to conceive
  *Kanojo wa karada no kekkan de **ninshin-dekinai**.*
  She can't become pregnant due to physical problems.

chūdoku-suru 中毒する *chūdoku* (poisoning, intoxication) + *suru*
- to get poisoned, to suffer poisoning
  *Shōnen wa kinoko de **chūdoku-shimashita**.*
  The boy was poisoned by a mushroom.

chiryō-suru 治療する *chiryō* (treatment, remedy) + *suru*
- to treat, to remedy
  *Kanojo wa kono byōin de kega o **chiryō-shite** moratta.*
  She had her injuries treated at this hospital.

kaifuku-suru 回復する *kaifuku* (recovery, recuperation) + *suru*
- to recover, to recuperate
  *Sofu wa mada shinzō hossa kara **kaifuku-shite imasen**.*
  My grandfather has not recovered yet from his heart attack.

9

Discussing Politics

THE SITUATION

Politics. Where to begin in that tangled web? Let's follow the political life of a politician from the very moment the candidate announces his intention to *rikkōho-suru* (run for election). Naturally, a candidate must *senkyo-undō-suru* (conduct an election campaign). In campaigning, it's important for him to be able to *enzetsu-suru* (make a speech) effectively. Unlike American senators, however, bashing certain other countries is not an effective means to win voters' support in Japan. Instead, a substantial part of the overall election campaign here seems to require the candidate to *junkai-suru* (cruise, run around) in a campaign car and to *renko-suru* (shout repeatedly) his name via a loudspeaker.

Again, unlike in America, candidates normally do not *hihan-suru* (criticize) other candidates' defects or char-

acter flaws. Candidates will simply *yakusoku-suru* (prom-
ise) to *kaiketsu-suru* (solve) any and all problems in
abstract ways. Candidates also frequently announce that
they either *hantai-suru* (oppose, object to) or *sansei-suru*
(support, agree with) certain controversial bills.

Finally the time comes for the public to *tōhyō-suru*
(vote). Some candidates will *tōsen-suru* (be elected) and
some will *rakusen-suru* (not be elected). At the election
campaign offices of the successful candidates, supporters
will *shūgō-suru* (gather) and *kanpai-suru* (make a toast)
with *sake*. All the campaign workers will *banzai-suru*
(cheer). Sooner or later reporters will come and *kaiken-
suru* (interview) the successful candidates.

With the hard race behind them, today's winners—
yesterday's ordinary people—are suddenly to *sonkei-
sareru* (be respected) as *sensei* (teacher, master). Many
of them will start immediately to *kashin-suru* (over-esti-
mate) their capacities and *jiman-suru* (boast) of their skill
and future glories. The unsuccessful candidates, on the
other hand, will *kansha-suru* (thank) everyone for the
kind support given to them, even though they must undoubtedly *rakutan-suru* (be discouraged).

Soon groups of supporters will go to the politician's
Tokyo offices in order to *chinjō-suru* (lodge a petition,
make a plea). Supporters are normally expected to *kenkin-
suru* (contribute money) to members of the Diet for their
political activities. The Diet members are obliged to
keichō-suru (listen) to their requests. They typically an-

swer that they will *kentō-suru* (discuss, study) and *zensho-suru* (try to improve) the situation. In return, of course, lobbyists must not forget to *senden-suru* (publicize) the politician's great efforts.

In reality, the office holders often *mushi-suru* (ignore, disregard) the requests.

If a Diet member is able to become the pet of an influential politician, he may *nyūkaku-suru* (enter the cabinet as a minister). As he is able to gain skill as a Diet member, he too will be able to *inemuri-suru* (take a nap) during sessions and *kanyo-suru* (be involved) in pay-off scandals.

As a result, the police will *taiho-suru* (arrest) him—that is if he is not to *nyūin-suru* (be hospitalized), as some politicians do in Japan. He will definitely *hitei-suru* (deny) his involvement and say that it has always been his secretary's secret vice to *juryō-suru* (accept) dirty money and to fail to *hōkoku-suru* (report) it to his superiors. The Diet will still *kanmon-suru* (summon) him. At last he will be obliged to *jinin-suru* (resign) from his ministerial post and *ritō-suru* (leave the party). Ho hum. Another day in Japanese politics.

DIALOGUE

MARY: *Ano hito wa kuruma no ue de nani o shite iru no desu ka?*
What is that man doing on top of that car?

MASAO: *Kare wa senkyo ni **rikkōho-shite**, **enzetsu-shite iru** no desu yo.*
He's running for the election and is making a speech.

MARY: *Kare wa nani o **apiiru-shiyō** to shite imasu ka?*
What's he making an appeal for?

MASAO: *Seiji o **kaikaku-shinakereba naranai** to itte imasu. Kore o **shuchō-shinai** to **tōsen-shinai** no desu. Daremo **rakusen-shitakunai** desu kara ne.*
He says that we must reform politics. If he doesn't assert this, he won't succeed in the election. No one wants to lose the election.

MARY: *Takusan no seijika ga oshoku de **kiso-sarete**, tsugi kara tsugi to **taiho-saremashita**. Kokumin wa seiji kaikaku yori mo oshoku o **bōshi-suru** koto o ichiban **kibō-shite iru** yō desu ga. Sō ja nai no desu ka?*
Many politicians were charged with bribery and arrested one after another. People want first of all to prevent bribery rather than political reform. Isn't that so?

MASAO: *Sono tōri desu ga, seijika wa oshoku bōshi o seiji kaikaku ni **tōgō-shita** node, oshoku bōshi mondai wa **shōmetsu-shita** yō ni narimashita.*
You're right, but politicians integrated the prevention of bribery into that of political reform, so that

the bribery prevention issue seems to have disappeared.

MARY: *Ā, naruhodo. Tokorode Nihon de wa gaikokujin wa **tōhyō-suru** kenri ga arimasu ka?*

Oh, really? By the way, do foreigners have the right to vote in Japan?

MASAO: *Hotondo no kuni to onaji yō ni, gaikokujin wa kokusei ni **sanka-suru** koto wa dekimasen. Shikashi iken o **happyō-suru** koto wa jiyū desu.*

As in most countries, foreigners can't take part in the politics of the country. But you're free to express your opinions.

MARY: *Sate, saikin no ichiban ōkina Nihon no seiji mondai no hitotsu wa kome no yunyū da to omoimasu. Kono saikin no hōan wa gikai o **tsūka-suru** to omoimasu ka?*

Well, I think one of Japan's greatest recent political issues is the import of rice. Do you think this recent bill will pass in the National Diet?

MASAO: *Sono mondai wa kokkai de nagai aida **shingi-sarete** kimashita. Shikashi Urugai Raundo o **seiko-saseru** tame, Nihon mo **kyōryoku-suru** koto o **yoginaku-sarete imasu** kara, tsūka-suru mitai desu ne.*

That issue has long been discussed in the Diet. But in order to make the Uruguay Round succeed, Japan is obliged to cooperate, so it looks like it might pass this time.

MARY: *Yatō wa **hantai-shite imasu** ga, daitasū ga **sansei-sureba**, hōan wa **kaketsu-saremasu**. Moshikasuruto kokkai wa **kaisan-suru** kamoshiremasen ne.*
The opposition parties oppose it, but if the majority agree, the bill will be approved. The chances are that the National Diet may be dissolved, right?

MASAO: *Tabun ne. Jikan o kakete mite minaito ikenai deshō.*
Maybe. I guess we'll just have to wait and see.

STRUCTURES AND SYNONYMS

rikkōho-suru 立候補する *rikkōho* (candidacy) + *suru*
• to run for election, to be a candidate
   Compare with *senkyo ni deru* 選挙に出る to run for an election, to be a candidate in an election
   *Kare wa **senkyo ni dereba**, tōsen-suru darō.*
   If he runs for election, he will be successful.

enzetsu-suru 演説する *enzetsu* (speech, address) + *suru*
• to make a speech, to give an address
   Compare with *kōen-suru* 講演する to deliver a speech, to make an address

*Kare wa **enzetsu-shinai** keredomo, mai kai tōsen-suru.*

He never makes a speech, but he is always successful in the elections.

apiiru-suru アピールする *apiiru* (appeal) + *suru*
- to appeal to/for, to make an appeal
  Compare with *uttaeru* 訴える to appeal to, to make an appeal
  *Demotai wa genpatsu kinshi o **uttaeta**.*
  The demonstrators made an appeal for the ban of nuclear power stations.

kaikaku-suru 改革する *kaikaku* (reform, correction) + *suru*
- to reform, to correct
  Compare with *aratameru* 改める to reform, to correct
  *Warui kanshū wa **aratameneba** naranai.*
  We have to correct bad habits.

shuchō-suru 主張する *shuchō* (assertion, allegation, claim) + *suru*
- to assert, to allege, to claim
  Compare with *iiharu* 言い張る to assert, to claim, to insist on
  *Kanojo wa sore ga uso de wa nai to **iiharu** kamoshiremasen.*
  She may assert that it's not a lie.

tōsen-suru 当選する *tōsen* (win an election, be elected) + *suru*
- to win an election, to be elected
  Compare with *erabareru* 選ばれる to be elected
  *Haha wa senkyo de kokkai giin ni **erabareta**.*
  My mom was elected as a National Diet member.

rakusen-suru 落選する *rakusen* (failure in the election) + *suru*
- to fail in the election
  Compare with *ochiru* 落ちる to fail in the election
  *Kondo senkyo de **ochireba**, kare wa seikai kara intai-suru darō.*
  If he fails in the election this time, he'll retire from the political world.

kiso-suru 起訴する *kiso* (indictment, accusation) + *suru*
- to indict, to accuse
  Compare with *uttaeru* 訴える to indict, to accuse, to prosecute
  *Kare wa anata o supai no tsumi de **uttaemashita**.*
  He indicted you on a charge of espionage.

taiho-suru 逮捕する *taiho* (capture, arrest) + *suru*
- to capture, to arrest
  Compare with *toraeru* 捕らえる to apprehend, to arrest
  *Satsujinsha wa Osaka de **toraerareta**.*
  The killer was arrested in Osaka.

bōshi-suru 防止する *bōshi* (prevention) + *suru*
- to prevent
  Compare with *fusegu* 防ぐ to prevent
  Suigai o fusegu tame, takai teibō ga tsukurareta.
  In order to prevent floods, high banks were constructed.

kibō-suru 希望する *kibō* (hope, expectation) + *suru*
- to hope, to expect
  Compare with *nozomu* 望む to hope, to expect
  Moshi kanojo ga watashi ga pātii ni sanka-suru koto o nozomunara, yorokonde sō shimasu.
  If she hopes that I'll attend her party, I'm glad to do so

tōgō-suru 統合する *tōgō* (unification, integration) + *suru*
- to unify, to integrate
  Compare with *matome awaseru* まとめ合わせる to unify, to integrate
  Watashitachi no shi wa go-ka-chōson o matome awasete tanjō-shimashita.
  Our city was born by unifying five towns and villages.

shōmetsu-suru 消滅する *shōmetsu* (disappearance) + *suru*
- to disappear
  Compare with *kiesaru* 消え去る to disappear
  Kinō no yuki wa mō kiesatte iru.
  Yesterday's snow has now disappeared.

tōhyō-suru 投票する *tōhyō* (vote, poll) + *suru*
• to vote, to poll, to ballot
Compare with *ireru* 入れる to give one's vote to someone, to vote
*Kare no kazoku wa zen'in Hara-san ni **ireru** darō.*
All his family members will vote for Mr. Hara.

tsūka-suru 通過する *tsūka* (passage) + *suru*
• to pass
Compare with *tōru* 通る to pass
*Seiji kaikaku hōan wa shūgiin o **tōranakatta**.*
The political reform bill did not pass the House of Representatives.

shingi-suru 審議する *shingi* (discussion, review) + *suru*
• to discuss, to review
Compare with *hanashi au* 話し合う to discuss
*Kokkai de atarashii nenkin seido o **hanashi atte iru.***
The Diet is discussing the new pension system.

seikō-suru 成功する *seikō* (success) + *suru*
• to succeed
Compare with *umaku yuku* うまく行く to succeed
*Kare no atarashii shōbai wa **umaku yukanakatta**.*
He did not succeed in his new business.

yoginaku-suru 余儀無くする *yoginaku* (oblige, compel) + *suru*
• to oblige, to compel

Compare with *yamuoenai* やむを得ない to be un-avoidable, to be obligatory

*Kare ga kanojo to rikon-suru koto wa **yamuoenakatta**.*

It was unavoidable for him to divorce her.

hantai-suru 反対する *hantai* (opposition, objection) + *suru*

• to oppose, to object

Compare with *sakarau* 逆らう to oppose, to cross, to disagree

*Shinmai wa buchō no hōshin ni **sakaratte** kubi ni natta.*

The newcomer opposed the manager's policy and was fired

sansei-suru 賛成する *sansei* (agreement) + *suru*

• to agree

Compare with *dōi-suru* 同意する to agree

*Kare no an ni **dōi-shimashita**.*

I agreed to his proposition.

kaketsu-suru 可決する *kaketsu* (approval, passage) + *suru*

• to approve, to pass

Compare with *tōru* 通る to approve, to pass

*Kokumin no tsuyoi hantai nimo kakawarazu, shōhizei hōan wa tsuini ryōin o **tōtta**.*

In spite of people's strong opposition, the consumption tax bill finally passed both the Houses.

kaisan-suru 解散する *kaisan* (dissolution) + *suru*
• to dissolve

FOR FURTHER STUDY

kenkin-suru 献金する *kenkin* (contribution, donation) + *suru*
• to contribute, to donate
    Wagasha wa yūryoku na seijika ni kanari no kane o **kenkin-shita**.
    Our company contributed a sizeable amount of money to the influential politician.

sōsaku-suru 捜索する *sōsaku* (search, investigation) + *suru*
• to search, to investigate
    Keisatsu wa kankei shorui o **sōsaku-suru** *tame seijika no uchi o hōmon-shita*.
    The police visited the politician's house to search for the documents concerned.

bakuro-suru 暴露する *bakuro* (exposure, disclosure) + *suru*
• to expose, to disclose, to reveal
    Shūkanshi wa geisha to daijin no kankei o **bakuro-shita**.
    The weekly magazine disclosed the minister's relation with a geisha.

hitei-suru 否定する *hitei* (negation, denial) + *suru*

• to deny, to renounce, to refute

Nikuson daitōryō wa Uōtāgēto jiken e no kanyo o **hitei-shimashita**.

President Nixon denied his involvement in the Watergate scandal.

10

Visiting a Japanese Home

THE SITUATION

Sometimes called a "rabbit hutch" by Europeans, most Japanese homes are relatively small. This is due to the limited space available for a comparatively large population, which in turn results in terribly high land prices. Some specialists say that with the money for which we *baikyaku-suru* (sell) Japan's land we could *kōnyū-suru* (purchase) the United States five times over. As you see, it is quite natural for most Japanese people to *chūcho-suru* (hesitate) to *shōtai-suru* (invite) you to his or her house. The result is that many foreigners will *taizai-suru* (stay) a long time in Japan without ever having a chance to *hōmon-suru* (visit) a Japanese home. If you have already been fortunate enough to *keiken-suru* (experience) such, you are one of a few lucky foreigners in Japan. When you get acquainted with a Japanese person, he or she may say *Asobi ni kite kudasai* (Please come to our home), without any definite date and time proposed. Often it may be a mere salutation meant to *hyōgen-suru* (express) a feeling of friendship or intimacy. It may not necessarily *imi-suru* (mean) an actual invitation. In fact, most or all of them who say so sincerely intend to *shōtai-suru* (invite) you, but due to the above reasons, they may *tōwaku-suru* (be embarrassed) when it comes to the actual situation. Of course, many people do mean what they say and *kibō-suru* (hope) you can visit soon. They will *teian-suru* (propose, suggest) a definite date and time. If you are not available on the suggested day, you can *enki-suru* (postpone) the date or *henkō-suru* (change) the time of your visit. If you cannot *kettei-suru* (decide) immediately, you should *renraku-suru* (contact) them later.

If a Japanese person does invite someone after all, it normally becomes a gorgeous affair beyond his or her economic capacities. Japanese guests are *ninshiki-suru* (aware) of this trend and *doryoku-suru* (make an effort) to *hoshō-suru* (compensate) the economic sacrifices of the host or hostess. This has created a custom in which a guest will *jisan-suru* (bring) a souvenir in order to *henrei-suru* (repay, return) the hospitality. You may *shinpai-suru* (be worried) about what to *sentaku-suru* (choose) as a proper souvenir for such an occasion. Well, a package of something to eat or drink, such as chocolate, candies or cookies, a bottle of whisky, or a dozen bottles of beer will be enough. When you *tōchaku-suru* (arrive) at the house, push the door bell. Someone will appear and *aisatsu-suru* (greet) you. You must *ojigi-suru* (bow) or *akushu-suru* (shake hands). Some Japanese people may even *aisatsu-suru* (greet) you again in a formal way with their hands placed on the tatami, bowing when you *chakuseki-suru* (sit down). You can just *mane-suru* (imitate) what they do. Following this formal greeting, you *purezento-suru* (present) your souvenir.

After a pleasant visit, when you find yourselves full of food and drink, and with nothing more to talk about, *shitsurei-suru* (leave), being sure to give thanks all around and marking your calender for the next time you can get together. Maybe the next party will be at your place!

DIALOGUE

MASAO: *Watashi no ie ni yōkoso oide kudasaimashita. Watashi no tsuma o **shōkai-itashimasu**. Kochira ga Miho desu. Miho, kochira ga onaji kaisha ni **kinmu-shite iru** Merii Jakuson-san.*
Welcome to my house. Let me introduce my wife. This is Miho. Miho, this is Mary Jackson who works with me at the company.

MARY: *Hajimemashite. Yoroshiku onegai itashimasu.*
It's a pleasure to meet you.

MIHO: *Kochira koso. Itsu **rainichi-saremashita** ka?*
The pleasure is mine. When did you come to Japan?

MARY: *Mō ichinen hodo Nihon ni **zaijū-shite imasu**. Demo Nihon no katei o **hōmon-suru** no wa hajimete desu node chotto **kōfun-shite imasu**.*

I've lived here for about a year, but this is the first time for me to visit a Japanese home, so I'm pretty excited about it.

MIHO: ***Anshin-shite** kudasai. **Shinpai-suru** hitsuyō wa arimasen. Kihonteki na koto wa amari **henka-shi-masen**.*

Rest assured. There's no need to worry. Basic things don't change much.

MARY: *Sō rashii desu ne. Tatoeba Nihon ni kuru mae wa **aisatsu-suru** toki, Nihonjin wa **ojigi suru** dake to kiite orimashita ga, jissai ni wa takusan no hito ga **akushu-suru** no o mite imasu yo. Shikashi ippanteki ni wa, jiko **hyōgen-suru** no ni, Nihonjin wa Yōroppa-jin yori mo kansetsuteki de aru yō ni omowaremasu ne.*

It seems that way, doesn't it. For example, before coming to Japan I heard that the Japanese just bow when greeting people, but actually I see lots of people shaking hands here. In general, though, Japanese people do seem more indirect than Europeans in expressing themselves.

MASAO: *Ē, kuni ni yotte shūkan to wa kanari **sōi-suru** mono desu ne. Demo tabun Merii-san wa uchi no*

*naka de wa kutsu o **shiyō-shinai** to iwareru koto ni*
***unzari-shiteiru** koto deshō ne.*

Well, customs do vary from one country to another.
But you're probably tired of people explaining how
we don't use shoes in the house, I'll bet.

MARY: *Sono tōri desu yo! Wā, kore wa kirei na uchi desu*
*ne. Itsu **kōnyū-sareta** no desu ka?*

That's for sure! Wow, this is a beautiful house.
When did you buy it?

MIHO: ***Kekkon-shita** chokugo desu. Watashitachi ga jissai*
*ni **sekkei-shita** no desu yo.*

Right after we got married. Actually, we designed it
ourselves.

MARY: *Hontō ni suteki desu ne.*

It's really lovely.

MASAO: *Arigatō. Nani ka nomimasen ka?*

Thanks! Won't you have a drink?

MIHO: *Otto wa **kinshu-shite imasu** node jūsu de **gaman-***
***suru** sō desu. Demo osoku **kitaku-suru** toki wa*
inshu-shite iru** yō desu. Honnin wa o-kyaku o **settai-
***suru** tame de aru to itte **benkai-shimasu** ga, kare no*
*iu koto wa **shinyō-dekimasen**.*

My husband is leaving off alcohol so he'll have to
be satisfied with juice. When he comes home late,

though, he seems to have had something to drink.
He makes excuses saying that it's to entertain his
customers, but I can't trust what he says.

MARY: *Honto desu ka? Jā, onnatachi wa biiru, Yamada-
san wa jūsu.*
Is that true? Then beer for the women and juice for
Mr. Yamada.

MASAO: *Sā, Merii-san o kangei-shite, kanpai-shimashō.*
Now then, to welcome Mary, let's drink a toast.

EVERYONE: *Kanpai!*
Cheers!

STRUCTURES AND SYNONYMS

shōkai-suru 紹介する *shōkai* (introduction, presentation)
+ *suru*
• to introduce, to present
Compare with *hikiawaseru* 引き合わせる to introduce
*Watashi no imōto o tomodachi ni **hikiawaseta**.*
I introduced my younger sister to a friend of mine.

kinmu-suru 勤務する *kinmu* (service, duty, work) + *suru*
• to serve, to be on duty, to work
Compare with *hataraku* 働く to work

*Kono kaisha de jūnen kan **hataraite imasu**.*
I've been working for this company for ten years.

rainichi-suru 来日する *rainichi* (visit to Japan) + *suru*
• to pay a visit to Japan, to come to Japan
  Compare with *Nihon ni kuru* 日本に来る to come to Japan
  ***Nihon ni kuru** toki, Hawai ni yorimashita.*
  I paid a visit to Hawaii when I came to Japan.

zaijū-suru 在住する *zaijū* (resident in/at) + *suru*
• to reside, to live
  Compare with *sumu* 住む to live, to reside
  *Chichi wa genzai Nihon ni **sunde inai.***
  My father does not live in Japan now.

hōmon-suru 訪問する *hōmon* (visit, call) + *suru*
• to pay a visit, to make a call
  Compare with *tazuneru* 訪ねる to visit, to call on
  *Anata o **tazunetara**, rusu deshita.*
  I visited you, but you were out.

kōfun-suru 興奮する *kōfun* (agitation, excitement) + *suru*
• to become agitated, to get excited
  Compare with *kanjō ga takaburu* 感情が高ぶる to get excited, to get worked up
  *Wareware no chiimu ga shiai ni katta node, minna **kanjō ga takabutte** imasu.*
  Because our team won the game, all of us are excited.

shinpai-suru 心配する *shinpai* (uneasiness, worry) + *suru*
• to feel uneasy, to worry
> Compare with *anjiru* 案じる to be anxious, to worry, to be concerned
> *Watashi no mi o **anjite**, haha ga denwa o kureta.*
> Being anxious about my safety, my mother called me.

henka-suru 変化する *henka* (variation, change) + *suru*
• to change, to vary
> Compare with *kawaru* 変わる to change
> *Kare no kangae wa kesshite **kawaranai** deshō.*
> His thinking will never change.

aisatsu-suru 挨拶する *aisatsu* (greeting, salutation) + *suru*
• to greet, to salute
> Compare with *eshaku-suru* 会釈する to bow
> *Yamada-san wa michi de au to watashi ni itsumo **eshaku-shimasu**.*
> Mrs. Yamada always bows to me when we meet on the street.

ojigi-suru お辞儀する (bowing) + *suru*
• to bow
> Compare with *atama o sageru* 頭を下げる to incline one's head, to bow
> *Seito wa watashi ni itsumo **atama o sagemasu**.*
> My pupils always bow to me.

akushu-suru 握手する *akushu* (shaking hands) + *suru*
- to shake hands
  Compare with *te o nigiru* 手を握る to shake hands
  *Kare wa watashi no **te o nigitte** arigatō to itta.*
  Shaking my hand, he said thanks.

hyōgen-suru 表現する *hyōgen* (expression, manifestation) + *suru*
- to express, to manifest
  Compare with *arawasu* 表す to express, to manifest
  *Kono e wa haru no yorokobi o yoku **arawashite iru**.*
  This painting expresses well the joy of spring.

kekkon-suru 結婚する *kekkon* (marriage, matrimony) + *suru*
- to marry, to enter into matrimony, wed
  Compare with *totsugu* 嫁ぐ to get married
  *Saikin de wa sanjū o sugite mo **totsuganai** josei ga kanari imasu.*
  Recently there are many women who aren't married even after thirty.

sekkei-suru 設計する *sekkei* (design) + *suru*
- to design

kinshu-suru 禁酒する *kinshu* (abstinence) + *suru*
- to abstain from drinking
  Compare with *sake o tatsu* 酒を断つ to stop drinking alcoholic beverages

*Isha wa chichi ni **sake o tate** to itta.*
The doctor told my father to stop drinking alcohol.

gaman-suru 我慢する *gaman* (patience, endurance, tolerance) + *suru*
• to be patient, to endure, to tolerate
    Compare with *taeru* 耐える to be patient, to endure, to stand
    *Kare wa kanojo no bujoku ni **taerarenakatta**.*
    He could not tolerate her insult.

kitaku-suru 帰宅する *kitaku* (homecoming) + *suru*
• to come home, to return home
    Compare with *uchi ni kaeru* 家に帰る to return home
    *Chichi wa mainichi osoku **uchi ni kaerimasu**.*
    My father comes home late every day.

inshu-suru 飲酒する *inshu* (drink) + *suru*
• to drink alcoholic beverages
    Compare with *nomu* 飲む to drink alcoholic beverages.
    *Kare wa amari **nomenai**.*
    He can't drink much.

settai-suru 接待する *settai* (entertainment, welcome) + *suru*
• to entertain, to welcome
    Compare with *motenasu* もてなす to entertain, to give hospitality

*Haha wa watashi no iinazuke o atsuku **motenashita**.*
My mother cordially entertained my fiancé.

benkai-suru 弁解する *benkai* (excuse, justification) + *suru*
- to make an excuse, to justify
  Compare with *ii wake-suru* 言い訳する to make an excuse, to justify
  ***Ii wake-suru** na!*
  Don't make excuses!

shinyō-suru 信用する *shinyō* (trust, confidence) + *suru*
- to trust, to place confidence in
  Compare with *shinjiru* 信じる to trust, to place confidence in
  *Shachō wa keiri kachō o zenmenteki ni **shinjite iru**.*
  The president totally trusts the accounting manager.

kangei-suru 歓迎する *kangei* (welcome) + *suru*
- to welcome

kanpai-suru 乾杯する *kanpai* (toast) + *suru*
- to drink a toast

FOR FURTHER STUDY

enryo-suru 遠慮する *enryo* (reservation, restraint) + *suru*
- to be reserved, to refrain from, to withhold
  *Kono heya de wa tabako o **enryo-shite** kudasai.*

Please refrain from smoking in this room.

chūcho-suru 躊躇する *chūcho* (hesitation, vacillation, irresolution) + *suru*
• to hesitate, to vacillate, to be irresolute
  *Kare wa watashi to kekkon-suru koto o **chūcho-shite iru**.*
  He hesitates to marry me.

shōtai-suru 招待する *shōtai* (invitation) + *suru*
• to invite
  *Kare wa watashi o yūshoku ni **shōtai-shimashita** ga, kotowarimashita.*
  He invited me to dinner, but I declined.

gokai-suru 誤解する *gokai* (misunderstand, misinterpret) + *suru*
• to misunderstand, to misinterpret
  *Kanojo wa watashi ga itta koto o **gokai-shita** yō da.*
  It seems to me that she misunderstood what I said to her.

11

Loanwords

LOANWORDS AND *SURU*

As already seen in previous chapters, loanwords from other languages can be used to form compound-*suru* verbs in Japanese. Some words in your native language, or in the foreign languages you already know, can be directly employed via the magical power of *suru,* as if they were original Japanese verbs. This fact will be a frequent advantage to foreign students of Japanese.

In Japanese, the parts of speech most used to create new verbs in combination with *suru* are nouns and adjectives. Let's briefly review some examples you should be familiar with by now.

NOUN + *SURU* = COMPOUND-*SURU* VERB
aisatsu-suru 挨拶する *aisatsu* (greeting) + *suru*
• to greet

aizu-suru 合図する *aizu* (sign, signal) + *suru*
• to give a signal or sign
kentō-suru 検討する *kentō* (an examination) + *suru*
• to examine or investigate

ADJECTIVE + *SURU* = COMPOUND-*SURU* VERB
akaku-suru 赤くする *akai* (red) + *suru*
• to make something red
takaku-suru 高くする *takai* (high) + *suru*
• to make something high
osoku-suru 遅くする *osoi* (slow) + *suru*
• to make something slow

However, not all nouns and adjectives are combinable with *suru*. This is the same for any loanword, as well. Whether or not a word can be combined with *suru* is very delicately related to its sound, meaning, and part of speech. Although there is no particular rule, through experience the native Japanese speaker, or dedicated student, develops a feel for whether or not certain Japanese words or loanwords are combinable with *suru* and whether they sound natural or unnatural.

It is important to note that other parts of speech are used to make loanword-*suru* combinations. That is, in addition to noun loanwords, such as *adobaisu-suru* (advise), *bakku-suru* (go back), *dēto-suru* (date), *memorii-suru* (memorize), many verb loanwords can be directly employed to combine with *suru*, as well.

LOANWORD VERB + *SURU* = COMPOUND-*SURU* VERB

akuseputo-suru アクセプトする *akuseputo* (accept) + *suru*
• to accept
arenji-suru アレンジする *arenji* (arrange) + *suru*
• to arrange
chekku-suru チェックする *chekku* (check) + *suru*
• to check

Furthermore, the gerund form of verb loanwords are often used, as in the following:

basshingu-suru バッシングする *basshingu* (bashing) + *suru*
• to bash
danpingu-suru ダンピングする *danpingu* (dumping) + *suru*
• to dump
jogingu-suru ジョギングする *jogingu* (jogging) + *suru*
• to jog
pitchingu-suru ピッチングする *pitchingu* (pitching) + *suru*
• to pitch

Here again there is no particular rule regarding whether you use a noun form, a regular verb, or a gerund form. These three forms are used case by case and therefore depend entirely on popular convention, sound, feeling, or context.

negoshiēshon-suru ネゴシエーションする and also *negoshiēto-suru*, but not the gerund form

kōdinēshon-suru コーデネイションする and also *kōdinēto-suru*, but not the gerund form

rizabēshon-suru リザベーションする and also *rizābu-suru,* but not the gerund form

akuseputo-suru アクセプトする but not the noun or gerund forms

arenji-suru アレンジする but not the noun or gerund forms

atatchi-suru アタッチする but not the noun or gerund forms

basshingu-suru バッシングする but rarely *basshu-suru*

runningu suru ランニングする but rarely *ran-suru*

English is not the only language to contribute words to Japanese. There are some loanwords derived from other foreign languages that are combinable with *suru* in the same manner as above. For example, from the German are *arubaito-suru* from *arbeiten* (work part-time), *essen-suru* from *essen* (eat), *trinken-suru* from *trinken* (drink), and *tanzen-suru* from *tanzen* (dance). French derivations include *torabāyu-suru* from *travail* (work), *bakansu-suru* from *vacance* (have a vacation), and *abanchūru-suru* from *aventure* (to have an amorous relationship or love affair).

Japan is currently very keen on internationalization, a fact reflected in the above contributions to the ongoing evolution of the Japanese language. Don't be provincial. Use loanwords as often as possible!

DIALOGUE

NOBUO: *Eigo o tsukatte Nihonjin to jiyū ni **komyunikēto-suru** hiketsu o shitte imasu ka?*
Do you know the secret of communicating freely with Japanese by using English words?

CHRIS: *Eigo o hanaseru Nihonjin to nara tōzen **komyu-nikēto-dekiru** deshō.*
It's quite natural for us to be able to communicate with Japanese people who speak English.

NOBUO: *Iya, Eigo o hanasanai ippan no Nihonjin to desu yo. Takusan no gairaigo to Nihongo no suru dōshi o **konbain-suru** to sugu fukugō dōshi o sakusei-suru koto ga dekimasu.*
No. With Japanese, in general, who don't speak English. You can produce compound-*suru* verbs by combining many loanwords with *suru*.

CHRIS: *Naruhodo. Rei o agete **setsumei-shite** kuremasen ka?*
I see. Will you explain it with some examples?

NOBUO: *Watashi ga **chekku-shita** tokoro ni yorimasu to, gairaigo dōshi to **konbain-suru** koto ga ōi yō desu. Amari nagai gairaigo wa mijikaku **katto-sarete** kara "suru" ga **konbain-saremasu**. Tatoeba, **ope-suru*** *wa "operation" ga **katto-sareta** ato de "suru" ga* **konbain-saremashita.**

According to what I checked, it's often combined with a loanword verb. If a loanword is too long, *suru* is combined after it has been cut short. For example, with *ope-suru*, *suru* was combined after "operation" was shortened.

CHRIS: *Sō ka. Ja, kawase rēto no hanashi ni **apurai-shite** mimashō.*

Aha. OK, let's actually apply it to a discussion about exchange rates.

NOBUO: *Doru no baryu ga saikin **uppu-shita** node, **depojitto-shinaide** en ni zenbu **konbāto-shita** hō ga yoi desu ne.*

Since the value of the dollar went up recently, it's better to convert everything to yen without depositing it.

CHRIS: *Shikashi **daun-suru** koto mo arimasu. Ekusuchenji rēto wa mainichi **chenji-shimasu** kara ne. Shōrai no ekusuchenji rēto o **esutimēto-suru** koto wa taihen muzukashii desu.*

But it can also go down. The exchange rate changes every day. It's really difficult to estimate future exchange rates.

NOBUO: *Sō desu yo. Sakunen doru no bāryū ga totsuzen* **doroppu-shita** *toki, hyaku doru* **rosu-shimashita**. *Demo* **abarēji-suru** *to umaku* **baransu-sarete iru** *yō desu.*

Exactly. Last year when the value of the dollar dropped suddenly, I lost a hundred dollars. But if I average it all, it seems to come out evenly balanced.

CHRIS: *Ā so. Futokoro guai ni mondai ga nakereba, konshū no uiikuendo wa watashitachi to tsukiatte kuremasen ka? Nikkō de* **kyanpu-suru** *yotei desu node. Tento wa sudeni* **arenji-shimashita** *shi jibuntachi de* **kukkingu-shimasu**.

So if your finances are OK now, how about joining us this weekend? We're planning to go camping in Nikko. We already arranged a tent and we'll cook by ourselves.

NOBUO: *Sore wa ii ne! Kanojo to* **dēto-suru** *yotei deshita ga, kanojo mo* **inbaito-shite** *ii desu ka?*

That's nice! I have a date with my girlfriend, but is it OK to invite her, too?

CHRIS: *Mochiron kanojo mo* **uerukamu-shimasu** *yo. Zehi* **pusshu-shite** *kudasai.*

Of course, we'll welcome her. Please push her to come, by all means.

NOBUO: *Ima sugu **teru-shite konfāmu-shimasu**. Tabun ōkē-suru deshō.*
I'll call her right away and confirm. I think she'll say OK.

CHRIS: *Honto? Yokatta! Kore de zenbu kimatta ne.*
Really? Great! Then we're all set.

STRUCTURES AND SYNONYMS

komyunikēto-suru コミュニケートする *komyunikēto* (communication) + *suru*
• to communicate
 Compare with *ishisotsū-suru* 意思疎通する to communicate
 *Kare wa gaikokujin no tsuma to **ishisotsū-dekinai**.*
 He can't communicate well with his foreign wife.

chekku-suru チェックする *chekku* (check) + *suru*
• to check
 Compare with *shiraberu* 調べる to check
 *Chūmon yōshi o **shirabete** kudasai.*
 Please check the order sheet.

konbain-suru コンバインする *konbain* (combine) + *suru*
• to combine
 Compare with *kumi awaseru* 組あわせる to combine

*Rajio kasetto tēpu rekōdā wa tēpu rekōdā to rajio o **kumi awasete** tsukurareta.*
The radio cassette tape-recorder was made by combining a tape-recorder with a radio.

ope-suru オペする *ope* (operation, operate) + *suru*
• to operate, to be operated on
Compare with *shujutsu-suru* 手術する to operate
*Kono kanja wa asu **shujutsu-shimasu**.*
This patient will undergo an operation tomorrow.

katto-suru カットする *katto* (cut) + *suru*
• to cut
Compare with *kiru* 切る to cut
*Kami o mijikaku **kitte** kudasai.*
Please cut my hair short.

apurai-suru アプライする *apurai* (apply) + *suru*
• to apply
Compare with *atehameru* 当てはめる to apply
*Kare no jiken wa jūsan jō ni **atehamaranai**.*
His case does not apply to Article 13.

appu-suru アップする *appu* (up, going up) + *suru*
• to go up, to increase
Compare with *agaru* 上がる to go up, to increase
*Nihon de wa kyūryō wa shigatsu ni **agarimasu**.*
In Japan, our salary is increased in April.

depojitto-suru デポジットする *depojitto* (deposit) + *suru*
* to deposit

> Compare with *azukeru* 預ける to deposit
> *Ano seijika wa Suisu no ginkō ni takusan okane o azuketa sō desu.*
> They say that the politician deposited a great deal of money in a Swiss bank.

konbāto-suru コンバートする *konbāto* (convert) + *suru*
* to convert

> Compare with *kaeru* 変える to convert
> *Nihyaku doru o en ni kaete kudasai.*
> Please convert two hundred dollars into yen.

daun-suru ダウンする *daun* (down, going down) + *suru*
* to go down, to decrease

> Compare with *sagaru* 下がる to go down, to decrease, to hang down
> *Tōkyō no chika wa juppāsento sagarimashita.*
> The land price in Tokyo has decreased by ten percent.

chenji-suru チェンジする *chenji* (change) + *suru*
* to change

> Compare with *kawaru* 変わる to change
> *Konya made ni ame wa yuki ni kawaru to kikimashita.*
> I heard the rain will change to snow by tonight.

esutimeito-suru エスティメイトする *esutimeito* (estimate) + *suru*
- to estimate

> Compare with *mitsumoru* 見積もる to estimate, to
> make an estimate
> *Kare wa itsumo yori takaku kōjihi o **mitsumoru** yō ni
> meirei-sareta.*
> He was ordered to estimate the construction costs
> higher than usual.

doroppu-suru ドロップする *doroppu* (drop) + *suru*
- to drop

> Compare with *sagaru* 下がる to drop; *daun-suru* ダ
> ウンする to go down
> *Doru no kachi wa **sagatta**.*
> The value of the dollar went down.

rosu-suru ロスする *rosu* (loss) + *suru*
- to lose

> *Rūzu-suru* (lose) is rarely used.
> Compare with *son-suru* 損する to lose, to suffer losses
> *Atarashii shigoto de **son-suru** kamo shiremasen.*
> I may suffer losses in my new business.

aberēji-suru アベレージする *aberēji* (average) + *suru*
- to average

> Compare with *heikin-suru* 平均する to average
> *Nenkan uriage gaku o **heikin-shite** kudasai.*
> Please average the total annual sales amount.

baransu-suru バランスする *baransu* (balance) + *suru*
• to balance
    Compare with *tsuriau* 釣り合う to balance
    *Kanojo no gōkana seikatsu wa shūnyū to **tsuriawanai**.*
    Her extravagant lifestyle does not balance with her
    income.

kyanpu-suru キャンプする *kyanpu* (camp) + *suru*
• to camp
    Compare with *yaei-suru* 野営する to camp
    *Tozan pātii wa hyōga de **yaei-seneba** naranakatta.*
    The mountaineering party had to camp on the glacier.

arenji-suru アレンジする *arenji* (arrange) + *suru*
• to arrange
    Compare with *tehai-suru* 手配する to arrange
    *Kare wa watashi no apāto o **tehai-shite** kureta.*
    He arranged my apartment house.

kukkingu-suru クッキングする *kukkingu* (cook) + *suru*
• to cook
    *Kukku-suru (to cook) is rarely used.
    Compare with *ryōri-suru* 料理する to cook
    *Watashi wa uchi de **ryōri** o tanoshimimasu.*
    I enjoy cooking at home.

dēto-suru デートする *dēto* (date) + *suru*
• to date
    Compare with *aibiki-suru* 逢引する to date

*Ano futari wa tonarimachi de **aibiki-shite iru** to kikimasu.*
I hear that the two are secretly dating in the next town.

inbaito-suru インバイトする *inbaito* (invite) + *suru*
• to invite
Compare with *maneku* 招く to invite
*Kinō kanojo ni shokuji ni **manekaremashita**.*
Yesterday I was invited to dinner by her.

uerukamu-suru ウエルカムする *uerukamu* (welcome) + *suru*
• to welcome
Compare with *kangei-suru* 歓迎する to welcome
*Kanojo wa bijin dakara doko ni ittemo **kangei-saremasu**.*
She is such a beauty that she's welcomed wherever she goes.

pusshu-suru プッシュする *pusshu* (push) + *suru*
• to push
Compare with *susumeru* 勧める to recommend
*Oji wa watashi ni daigaku ni yuku yō ni **susumeta**.*
My uncle urged me to go to college.

teru-suru テルする *teru* (telephone) + *suru*
• to telephone
Compare with *denwa-suru* 電話する to telephone

*Haha no hi ni haha ni **denwa-shita**.*
I called Mom on mother's day.

konfāmu-suru コンファームする *konfāmu* (confirm) +
suru
• to confirm
Compare with *kakunin-suru* 確認する to confirm, to
check
*Kippu ga toreta ka **kakunin-suru** hitsuyō ga arimasu.*
I need to confirm that the ticket was available.

ōkē-suru オーケーする *ōkē* (OK) + *suru*
• to okay, to approve or endorse
Compare with *ukeireru* 受け入れる to okay, to say
yes
*Kanojo wa watashi no shōtai o **ukeirenai** darō.*
She will probably not accept my invitation.

FOR FURTHER STUDY

baito-suru バイトする *baito* (shortened form of the German verb *arbeiten,* "to work," meaning a part-time job)
+ *suru*
• to have a part-time job
*Kono gakusei wa shū ni kai **baito-shite imasu.***
This student has a part-time job twice a week.

ajasuto-suru アジャストする *ajasuto* (adjustment) + *suru*
• to adjust

*Rōpu no nagasa o **ajasuto-shimashō**.*
Let's adjust the length of the rope.

dokkingu-suru ドッキングする *dokkingu* (dock) + *suru*
• to dock
*Uchūsen wa jikken-shitsu ni **dokkingu-shimasu**.*
The space ship will dock with the experimental chamber.

janpu-suru ジャンプする *janpu* (jump) + *suru*
• to jump
*Shōnen wa ringo o toru tame ni takaku **janpu-shimashita**.*
The little boy jumped high to pick an apple.

12
Onomatopoeia

ONOMATOPOEIA AND *SURU*

In addition to all the other usages you've come to know and love, *suru* can also be combined with (1) onomatopoeic words expressing the sound a particular subject makes (the subject itself is often omitted in normal phrases), and (2) onomatopoeic adverbs showing a particular subject's state of being. Unlike previous cases, *suru* here acquires the following meanings:

(a) to make, or to describe a particular sound

(b) to be in, or to describe a particular state of being

In the latter case, the onomatopoeic adverb is roughly equivalent to verbs meaning "to feel," "to stay," "to be," and "to remain." As such, they may well be considered as adjectives or adjectival equivalents, as in the following examples:

(a) Onomatopoeia + *suru*: to express or describe particular sounds

pata-pata-suru ぱたぱた *pata-pata* (tip-tap, pitter-patter, flap-flap) + *suru*

• to flap, to flutter, to patter
  Applicable to the sounds of thin and flat things like flags, sails, handkerchieves.

goro-goro-suru ごろごろ *goro-goro* (rumble, roll, thunder) + *suru*

• to rumble, to roll, to thunder
  Applicable to the sound of thunder or of heavy rolling things like old carts, stones, bowling balls, and beer barrels.

(b) Onomatopoeic adverb + *suru*: to express particular states

hara-hara-suru はらはら *hara-hara* (uneasy, insecure) + *suru*

• to feel uneasy, to feel insecure
  Applicable to states of uneasiness, insecurity, or dangerous situations.

waku-waku-suru わくわく *waku-waku* (excited, thrilled, heart-throbbing with happiness) + *suru*

• to be excited, to be thrilled, to be crazy about
  Applicable to states or feelings of excitement, happiness or delight.

Many onomatopoeic words combined with *suru* express both sounds and states of being, as in the case of *goro-goro-suru.* This phrase is normally used to express a sound as explained above. But *goro-goro-suru* can also be used to indicate the state of being idle, or of loafing around, as explained in (b). There are many other similar onomatopoeic expressions, but it is interesting to note that most of them are created by the repetition of the same sound, as in *waku-waku*, *sara-sara*, *ira-ira*, *hoku-hoku*, and so on. Almost all of these expressions can be safely combined with *suru* to obtain the aforementioned effects and meanings.

There are other types of onomatopoeic words and expressions that are not comprised of repeated sounds. Examples include *kakkō* (cuckoo), *bān* (bang), *gōn* (gong), *pasha* (splash), and *kachi* (click). Most of these are not directly combinable with *suru*. Therefore, special care must be taken when dealing with this type of onomatopoeia.

For the most part, however, onomatopoeia are easy and fun to use, adding a natural and vivacious tone to your speech. Don't *doki-doki-suru* (be nervous). Experiment and enjoy this creative and playful aspect of the Japanese language!

DIALOGUE

*Onomotopoeic compound verbs are indicated with an asterisk.

CHRIS: *Kesa **bōtto-shite** eki no hō ni **sanpo-shite** imashi-ta ga, **ukkari-shite** aka shingō o **mushi-shite** dōro* *o ōdan-shite ita no desu. Torakku no kyū burēki no oto ni *hatto-shite sutoppu-shimashita.*

This morning I was taking a walk toward the station *in a daze. *Forgetting myself, I crossed the road, disregarding the red light. *Startled by the sudden braking noise of the truck, I stopped.

NOBUO: *Torakku wa anata ni shōtotsu-shita no desu ka? Kega-shimasen deshita ka?*

Did the truck hit you? Weren't you hurt?

CHRIS: *Nan to torakku wa watashi no sū inchi mae de teisha-shite imashita. Untenshu wa *katto-shite, Bakayarō! to watashi o batō-shimashita. Fukaku ojigi-shite, nando mo shazai-shimashita ga, untenshu wa *puri-puri-shite watashi no fuchūi o hinanshi tsuzukemashita. Watashi wa *peko-peko-suru dake deshita.*

To my surprise, the truck stopped only a few inches in front of me. *Flying into a great rage, the driver berated me with "You fool!" I bowed deeply and apologized to him many times, but the driver was huffing with anger and continued to criticize my carelessness. I could do nothing but *bow over and over again.

NOBUO: *Kare wa okane o yōkyū-shimasen deshita ka? Kurisu-san ni ranbō-shimasen deshita ka? Tonikaku kare wa taihen bikkuri-shita yō desu ne.*

Didn't he ask you for money? Didn't he become violent toward you? Anyhow, he must have been awfully surprised.

CHRIS: *Watashi wa *biku-biku-shite imashita ga, kare wa ranbō-shimasen deshita. Yagate atari ga *wai-wai-shite iru koto ni kizukimashita. Shikashi dare mo watashi o enjo-shite kuremasen deshita. Patokā ga tōchaku-shita node, watashi wa *hotto-shimashi-ta.*

I was *scared silly, but he didn't become violent. In the meantime, I noticed people *making a fuss around us. Yet nobody helped me. A patrol car arrived, and I *breathed a sigh of relief.

NOBUO: *Sō deshō ne.*
I can imagine!

CHRIS: *Kare wa sairen no oto o kiite *sowa-sowa-shi hajime, soshite patokā ga sekkin-shite kuru no o mitara *gata-gata-shite, isoide tōsō-shite shimai-mashita.*

Hearing the sound of the siren, he began to *get uneasy; then seeing the patrol car approach, he be-gan *shaking and ran away quickly.

NOBUO: *Keisatsu wa mondai o dono yō ni kaiketsu-shita no desu ka?*
How did the police solve the problem?

CHRIS: *__Doki-doki-shinagara__ keikan ni __setsumei-shi-mashita__. Shikashi keikan wa shijū *__niko-niko-shite imashita__. Soshite kega ga nai koto o __kakunin-suru__ to, "Shingō ni __chūi-shite__ aruite kudasai" to itte, tachisarimashita._

I *felt my heart pounding as I explained the matter to the policeman. But the policeman was *smiling at me the whole time. After confirming that there were no injuries, he said, "Pay attention to the signals when walking," and went away.

NOBUO: _Rakkii desu ne!_

Lucky for you!

STRUCTURES AND SYNONYMS

*__bōtto-suru__ ぼうっとする _bōtto_ (dazed, stupefied) + _suru_
• to be in a daze, to be stupefied
 Compare with _hōshin-suru_ 放心する to be in a daze, to be stupefied
 _Kare wa uchi ga moete iru no o mite __hōshin-shite__ shimatta._
 Having seen his house burning, he was stupefied.

__sanpo-suru__ 散歩する _sanpo_ (take a walk, stroll) + _suru_
• to take a walk, to stroll
 Compare with _yūho-suru_ 遊歩する to take a walk, to stroll

*Sobo wa maiasa go-ji ni okite, **yūho-shimasu***.
Getting up at five every morning, my grandmother takes a stroll.

ukkari-suru うっかりする *ukkari* (absentminded, unconscious) + *suru*
• to be absentminded, to be unconscious

mushi-suru 無視する *mushi* (ignore, disregard) + *suru*
• to ignore, to disregard

ōdan-suru 横断する *ōdan* (cross, traverse) + *suru*
• to cross, to traverse
   Compare with *yoko giru* 横切る to cross, to traverse
   *Takusan no dōbutsu ga kono dōro o **yoko giru** node, chūi-shite kudasai.*
   Since many animals go across this road, please be careful.

hatto-suru はっとする *hatto* (be startled, be taken aback) + *suru*
• to be startled, to be taken aback

sutoppu-suru ストップする *sutoppu* (stop, discontinuation) + *suru*
• to stop, to discontinue
   Compare with *tomaru* 止まる to stop, to halt, to discontinue

*Kono kishu no seisan ga raigetsu kara **tomarimasu**.*
The production of this model will be discontinued next month.

shōtotsu-suru 衝突する *shōtotsu* (collision) + *suru*
• to collide
   Compare with *butsukaru* ぶつかる to collide
   *Kare no kuruma ga basu ni **butsukarimashita**.*
   His car collided with a bus.

kega-suru 怪我する *kega* (wound) + *suru*
• to be wounded
   Compare with *kizu ou* 傷を負う to be wounded, to be hurt
   *Kōtsū jiko de kanojo wa atama ni **kizu o otta**.*
   In the traffic accident, she was wounded on the head.

teisha-suru 停車する *teisha* (stoppage of a vehicle) + *suru*
• to stop a vehicle
   Compare with *tomeru* 止める to stop a vehicle
   *Mise no mae de **tomete** kudasai.*
   Please stop in front of the store.

katto-suru かっとする *katto* (fume, fly into a rage) + *suru*
• to fume, to fly into a rage
   Compare with *puri-puri-suru* (see below)

batō-suru 罵倒する *batō* (condemnation) + *suru*
- to condemn

  Compare with *nonoshiru* 罵る to condemn

  *Juken ni shippai-shita koto de chichi wa watashi o **nonoshitta**.*

  My father condemned me for failing the entrance exam.

shazai-suru 謝罪する *shazai* (apology) + *suru*
- to apologize, to make an apology

  Compare with *ayamaru* 謝る to apologize, to make an apology

  *Watashi wa mado garasu o kowashita koto o **ayamaraneba naranai**.*

  I must apologize for having broken the window.

*puri-puri-suru ぷりぷりする *puri-puri* (flare up in anger, fly into a great rage) + *suru*
- to flare up in anger, to fly into a great rage

  Compare with *pun-pun-suru* ぷんぷんする in anger, in a huff

  *Watashi ga okurete-kita node, kare wa **pun-pun-shite ita**.*

  Because I arrived late, he was angry.

hinan-suru 非難する *hinan* (criticism) + *suru*
- to criticize

  Compare with *semeru* 責める to criticize

*Haha wa watashi no iede o **semenakatta**.*
My mother didn't cricize me for running away from home.

*peko-peko-suru ぺこぺこする *peko-peko* (repetitive bowing) + *suru*
• to bow over and over, to bow repeatedly

ranbō-suru 乱暴する *ranbō* (violence) + *suru*
• to become violent
   Compare with *bōryoku o furū* 暴力を振るう to do violence to, to be violent
   *Furyō gakusei wa sensei ni **bōryoku o furutte**, taigaku-saserareta.*
   Having been violent towards his teacher, the bad student was dismissed from school.

bikkuri-suru びっくりする *bikkuri* (surprise) + *suru*
• to be surprised
   Compare with *odoroku* 驚く to be surprised
   *Sore o mite **odorokanaide** kudasai.*
   Don't be surprised when you see it.

*biku-biku-suru びくびくする *biku-biku* (be scared silly) + *suru*
• to be scared silly

*wai-wai-suru わいわいする *wai-wai* (make a fuss, make a lot of noise) + *suru*
• to make a fuss, to be noisy

Compare with *gaya-gaya-suru* がやがやする to make a fuss, to be noisy

Gaya-gaya-shinaide kiite kudasai.

Don't be noisy, and listen to me, please.

enjo-suru 援助する *enjo* (help, aid) + *suru*
• to help, to aid

Compare with *tasukeru* 助ける to help, to aid

Kanojo wa tasukete to sakenda.

"Help!" she shouted.

*hotto-suru ほっとする *hotto* (heave a sigh of relief, sigh with relief) + *suru*
• to heave a sigh of relief, to feel relieved

kaiketsu-suru 解決する *kaiketsu* (solution) + *suru*
• to solve

Compare with *katazukeru* かたづける to solve, to clean up

Daitōryō wa kokkyō mondai o katazukete, bessō de kyūyō-shite iru.

Having solved the border issue, the president is taking a rest at his villa.

*sowa-sowa-suru そわそわする *sowa-sowa* (agitation, uneasiness) + *suru*
• to feel agitated, to feel uneasy

sekkin-suru 接近する *sekkin* (approach) + *suru*
• to approach

Compare with *chikazuku* 近づく to approach
Kare wa dai gakusha da ga, chikazuki yasui.
He's a great scholar, but he's easy to approach.

*gata-gata-suru がたがたする *gata-gata* (chatter, shake)
+ *suru*
• to chatter, to shake

tōsō-suru 逃走する *tōsō* (escape) + *suru*
• to escape, to flee
Compare with *nigeru* 逃げる to escape, to run away
Koko kara nigereba, shasatsu-shimasu.
If you escape from here, I will shoot you.

*doki-doki-suru どきどきする *doki-doki* (pounding heart)
+ *suru*
• to feel one's heart pound, to be nervous

*niko-niko-suru にこにこする *niko-niko* (smile) + *suru*
• to smile

FOR FURTHER STUDY

*yura-yura-suru ゆらゆらする *yura-yura* (sway, waver,
flicker) + *suru*
• to sway, to waver, to flicker
Watashi no bōto wa nami de yura-yura-shite imasu.
My boat is swaying due to the waves.

mota-mota-suru もたもたする *mota-mota* (slow, tardy) + *suru*
• to be slow, to be tardy
    *Kanojo wa shigoto ga itsumo **mota-mota-shite iru.***
    She is always slow at work.

hayaku-suru 速くする / 早くする *hayaku* (rapid, early) + *suru*
• to make it rapid or early
    *Kaiten o **hayaku-suru** to shindō ga hageshiku narimasu.*
    If you make the rotation faster, the vibration becomes stronger.

takaku suru 高くする *takaku* (high, loud) + *suru*
• to make higher, to make louder
    *Supiikā no oto o **takaku-shite** kudasai.*
    Please make the speaker louder.

Appendix

Onomatopoeic compound verbs are indicated with an asterisk.

[A]

aberēji-suru アベレージする to average

aisatsu-suru 挨拶する to greet, to salute

aizu-suru 合図する to give a signal, to sign, to give a sign

ajasuto-suru アジャストする to adjust

ajitsuke-suru 味付けする to season, to flavor

akushu-suru 握手する to shake hands

anaunsu-suru アナウンスする to announce (via a loud-speaker)

anki-suru 暗記する to memorize, to learn by heart

annai-suru 案内する to guide, to lead

anshin-suru 安心する to rest assured, to feel at ease

apiiru-suru アピールする to appeal

appu-suru アップする to go up, to increase
apurai-suru アプライする to apply
arenji-suru アレンジする to arrange

[B]
baito-suru バイトする to do a part-time job
bakuro-suru 暴露する to expose, to disclose, to reveal
baransu-suru バランスする to balance
batō-suru 罵倒する to rail, to condemn
benkai-suru 弁解する to make an excuse, to justify
benkyō-suru 勉強する to reduce, to discount
benkyō-suru 勉強する to study, to do one's lesson
bikkuri-suru びっくりする to be surprised
biku-biku-suru びくびくする to be scared silly
bōshi-suru 防止する to prevent, to check
*bōtto-suru ぼうっとする to be dazed, stupified

[C]
chekku-suru チェックする to check, to examine, to
    inspect
chekkuauto-suru チェックアウトする to check out
chikoku-suru 遅刻する to be late
chiryō-suru 治療する to treat, to remedy
chōka-suru 超過する to exceed, to surpass
chōsa-suru 調査する to do research, to survey, to inves-
    tigate
chūcho-suru 躊躇する to hesitate, to vacillate, to be
    irresolute
chūdoku-suru 中毒する to be poisoned

chūi-suru 注意する to take care of, to be careful, to be watchful, to be cautious

chūmon-suru 注文する to place an order, to request

chūsha-suru 駐車する to park

[D]

dannen-suru 断念する to give up, to abandon

daun-suru ダウンする to go down, to decrease

denwa-suru 電話する to telephone, to make a phone call

depojitto-suru デポジットする to deposit

dēto-suru デートする to date

*doki-doki-suru どきどきする to feel one's heart pounding

dokkingu-suru ドッキングする to dock

doroppu-suru ドロップする to drop

[E]

enjo-suru 援助する to help, to aid

enryo-suru 遠慮する to be reserved, to refrain from, to withhold

enzetsu-suru 演説する to make a speech, to give an address

esutimeito-suru エスティメイトする to estimate

[F]

fūin-suru 封印する to seal

fukuyō-suru 服用する to take medicine

funin-suru 赴任する to leave for one's new post

funshitsu-suru 紛失する to be lost, to lose

fusessei-suru 不節制する to be intemperate, to commit excesses

fusoku-suru 不足する to be short, to lack

[G]

gaishutsu-suru 外出する to go out

gaitō-suru 該当する to be applicable, to fall under

gaman-suru 我慢する to be patient, to endure, to tolerate

*gata-gata-suru がたがたする to chatter, to shiver, to shake

gesha-suru 下車する to get out of a vehicle, to alight

gizo-suru 偽造する to forge, to fabricate

gokai-suru 誤解する to misunderstand, to misinterpret

gōkaku-suru 合格する to pass a test, to be successful in an exam

[H]

haiken-suru 拝見する to look, to inspect

haishaku-suru 拝借する to borrow, to loan

haitatsu-suru 配達する to deliver

hakken-suru 発見する to discover, to find out

hakkō-suru 発行する to issue, to publish

hanbai-suru 販売する to sell, to market

hantai-suru 反対する to oppose, to object

happyō-suru 発表する to announce, to state, to publicize

hassei-suru 発生する to occur, to happen, to break out

hassō-suru 発送する to dispatch, to forward

*hatto-suru はっとする to startle, to be taken aback

hayaku-suru 速くする/早くする to make rapid or early

henji-suru 返事する to reply, to answer, to respond

henka-suru 変化する to change, to vary

hikaku-suru 比較する to compare

hinan-suru 非難する to criticize

hirō-suru 疲労する to be fatigued, to get tired

hitei-suru 否定する to deny, to renounce, to refute

hokan-suru 保管する to deposit, to store, to keep

hōmon-suru 訪問する to pay a visit, to make a call

hōmusutei-suru ホームステイする to home-stay, to stay at a private home

hoshō-suru 保証する to warrant, to guarantee

hōsō-suru 包装する to pack, to wrap

*hotto-suru ほっとする to heave a sigh of relief, to feel relieved

hyōgen-suru 表現する to express, to manifest

[I]

inbaito-suru インバイトする to invite

inshu-suru 飲酒する to drink alcoholic beverages

[J]

janpu-suru ジャンプする to jump

jikoshōkai-suru 自己紹介する to introduce oneself

jiman-suru 自慢する to boast, to brag

jisan-suru 持参する to bring, to carry

jōsha-suru 乗車する to get on/in a vehicle, to take a bus/train

jōshō-suru 上昇する to rise, to go up

jūji-suru 従事する to be occupied, to be engaged in

juken-suru 受験する to take a test, to take an exam

junbi-suru 準備する to prepare, to arrange

juryō-suru 受領する to receive, to get

jushin-suru 受信する to receive a signal/message

jūtai-suru 渋滞する to be delayed, to be late

[K]

kaifuku-suru 回復する to recover, to recuperate

kaihatsu-suru 開発する to develop

kaikaku-suru 改革する to reform, to correct

kaiketsu-suru 解決する to solve

kaimono-suru 買い物する to do shopping

kaisai-suru 開催する to hold, to open

kaisan-suru 解散する to dissolve

kaishi-suru 開始する to start, to begin

kaiten-suru 回転する to rotate, to revolve, to turn

kaitō-suru 解凍する to thaw, to defrost, to defreeze

kaitō-suru 回答する to answer, to respond, to solve

kaketsu-suru 可決する to approve, to pass

kakugo-suru 覚悟する to be ready, to be prepared

kakuhan-suru 攪拌する to stir, to churn

kakuho-suru 確保する to secure, to assure, to guarantee

kakunin-suru 確認する to confirm

kakutei-suru 確定する to be settled, to be decided

kanbyō-suru 看病する to nurse, to tend

kanchi-suru 完治する to recover completely, to be cured completely

kandan-suru 歓談する to have a pleasant chat, to enjoy a pleasant talk

kangei-suru 歓迎する to welcome

kankō-suru 観光する to see the sights, to tour

kanpai-suru 乾杯する to drink a toast

kanran-suru 観覧する to view, to watch, to see

kanryō-suru 完了する to complete, to conclude

karōshi-suru 過労死する to die due to overwork

katto-suru カットする to cut

*katto-suru かっとする to fly into a rage

kazei-suru 課税する to impose a tax, to tax

kega-suru 怪我する to be wounded, to be injured

keika-suru 経過する to elapse, to pass, to run

keikaku-suru 計画する to plan, to contemplate

keiken-suru 経験する to experience, to be experienced in

keisan-suru 計算する to calculate, to count

keizoku-suru 継続する to continue

kekkin-suru 欠勤する to be absent from work

kekkon-suru 結婚する to marry, to enter into matrimony, to wed

kenkin-suru 献金する to contribute, to donate

kensa-suru 検査する to inspect, to test, to examine

kenshin-suru 検診する to check, to examine

kettei-suru 決定する to decide, to determine

kibō-suru 希望する to hope, to expect

kikkoku-suru 帰国する to return to one's country
kinmu-suru 勤務する to serve, to be on duty, to work
kinshu-suru 禁酒する to abstain from drinking
kinyū-suru 記入する to write down, to fill in
kiroku-suru 記録する to record, to jot down
kisai-suru 記載する to note, to enter, to record
kisha-suru 帰社する to return to one's company
kiso-suru 起訴する to indict, to accuse, to prosecute
kitaku-suru 帰宅する to come home, to return home
kitei-suru 規定する to set forth, to prescribe
kōfun-suru 興奮する to get aroused, to get excited
kōkan-suru 交換する to exchange, to convert
komyunikēto-suru コミュニケートする to communicate
konbain-suru コンバインする to combine
konbāto-suru コンバートする to convert
konfāmu-suru コンファームする to confirm
kōnyū-suru 購入する to purchase, to acquire, to buy
konzatsu-suru 混雑する to be crowded, to be congested
kōryo-suru 考慮する to consider
kōshō-suru 交渉する to negotiate, to discuss
kukkingu-suru クッキングする to cook
kumiwake-suru 組分けする to divide into classes/groups
kyanpu-suru キャンプする to camp
kyanseru machi-suru キャンセル待ちする to wait for a cancellation
kyōryoku-suru 協力する to cooperate, to collaborate
kyōsō-suru 競争する to compete, to contest, to race
kyūkei-suru 休憩する to take a rest, to have a break

kyūyō-suru 休養する to take a rest, to repose

[M]

maebarai-suru 前払する to pay in advance

manetsu-suru 満悦する to eat or drink to one's full content, to enjoy fully

manzoku-suru 満足する to be satisfied, to be gratified, to be content

mensetsu-suru 面接する to meet, to have an interview

*mota-mota-suru もたもたする to be slow or tardy

mushi-suru 無視する to ignore, to disregard

[N]

neage-suru 値上げする to hike the price, to raise the price

nebiki-suru 値引きする to discount, to deduct the price

nesage-suru 値下げする to cut the price, to lower the price

*niko-niko-suru にこにこする to smile, to beat

ninshin-suru 妊娠する to become pregnant, to conceive

nōfu-suru 納付する to pay

nokku-suru ノックする to knock

nōnyū-suru 納入する to pay, to deliver

nōzei-suru 納税する to pay taxes

nyūgaku-suru 入学する to enter school/college/university, to be admitted to school/college/university

nyūin-suru 入院する to be hospitalized

nyūjō-suru 入場する to enter, to be admitted to

nyūkoku-suru 入国する to enter a country

nyūsha-suru 入社する to enter a company

nyūshitsu-suru 入室する to enter a room

nyūyoku-suru 入浴する to take a bath or shower, to bathe

[O]

ōbā-suru オーバーする to go over, to surpass, to exceed

ōdan-suru 横断する to cross, to traverse

ojigi-suru お辞儀する to bow

ōkē-suru オーケーする to okay, to say "yes"

ope-suru オペする to operate, to be operated

[P]

pējingu-suru ページングする to page

*peko-peko-suru ぺこぺこする to bow repeatedly

*puri-puri-suru ぷりぷりする to fly into a rage, to fume

pusshu-suru プッシュする to push

[R]

rainichi-suru 来日する to pay a visit to Japan, to come to Japan

raisha-suru 来社する to come to a company, to pay a visit to a company

rakusen-suru 落選する to fail in the election

ranbō-suru 乱暴する to do violence to

renraku-suru 連絡する to contact, to communicate, to get in touch with, to notify

rikai-suru 理解する to understand, to comprehend

rikkōho-suru 立候補する to run for an election, to be a candidate for an election

rosu-suru ロスする to lose

ryōri-suru 料理する to cook

ryōyō-suru 療養する to recuperate

[S]

sadō-suru 作動する to function, to operate, to work

sakugen-suru 削減する to reduce, to decrease, to cut

sakusei-suru 作成する to make, to prepare

sanka-suru 参加する to attend, to take part in

sanpo-suru 散歩する to take a walk, to stroll

sansei-suru 賛成する to agree, to approve

sanshō-suru 参照する to refer to, to consult

satsuei-suru 撮影する to take a picture, to photograph

seikō-suru 成功する to succeed

seisan-suru 精算する to settle an account

sekkei-suru 設計する to design

sekkin-suru 接近する to approach

senden-suru 宣伝する to advertise, to publicize

sentaku-suru 洗濯する to wash, to launder

sesshu-suru 摂取する to take in, to ingest

setsumei-suru 説明する to explain

setsuyaku-suru 節約する to save, to economize

setsuzoku-suru 接続する to link, to connect, to join

settai-suru 接待する to entertain, to welcome

settei-suru 設定する to fix, to establish, to set

shazai-suru 謝罪する to apologize, to make an apology

shibō-suru 死亡する to die, to perish

shigoto-suru 仕事する to work, to do one's job/task, to do business

shiji-suru 指示する to instruct, to direct, to order

shiken-suru 試験する to test, to examine, to give an examination

shinbō-suru 辛抱する to endure, to be patient, to forbear

shingi-suru 審議する to discuss, to review

shinkoku-suru 申告する to declare

shinpai-suru 心配する to be anxious, to worry

shinsei-suru 申請する to apply for

shinyō-suru 信用する to trust, to place confidence in

shitaku-suru 支度する to get ready, to make arrangements

shiyō-suru 使用する to utilize, to use, to make use of

shōkai-suru 紹介する to introduce

shokuji-suru 食事する to eat, to have a meal

shomei-suru 署名する to sign

shōmetsu-suru 消滅する to disappear

shōtai-suru 招待する to invite

shōtotsu-suru 衝突する to clash, to collide, to hit

shozoku-suru 所属する to belong to, to pertain to

shuccho-suru 出張する to travel on business, to make a business trip

shuchō-suru 主張する to assert, to claim

shūgō-suru 集合する to assemble, to gather

shujutsu-suru 手術する to undergo an operation, to perform an operation *shuppatsu-suru* 出発する to depart, to leave, to start

shūri-suru 修理する to repair, to mend

shūryō-suru 終了する to complete, to end, to finish

shussha-suru 出社する to come to one's company, to be present in the office

shutoku-suru 取得する to acquire, to get, to obtain

shūyō-suru 収容する to accommodate, to admit

sōbi-suru 装備する to equip, to be equipped, to feature

sōdan-suru 相談する to consult

sōfu-suru 送付する to send, to forward

sōi-suru 相違する to differ, to disagree, to vary

sōkin-suru 送金する to remit money

sōsa-suru 操作する to operate, to handle, to move

sōsaku-suru 捜索する to search, to investigate

sōtō-suru 相当する to correspond, to be proportionate

sotsugyō-suru 卒業する to graduate from

*sowa-sowa-suru そわそわする to feel uneasy, to feel agitated

sutoppu-suru ストップする to stop, to halt, to discontinue

[T]

taigaku-suru 退学する to be dismissed from school, to leave school

taiho-suru 逮捕する to capture, to arrest

taiin-suru 退院する to leave a hospital

taiki-suru 待機する to wait for, to await

tainin-suru 退任する to resign from a post

taisha-suru 退社する to leave one's office, to retire from a company

taishoku-suru 退職する to retire, to quit

taizai-suru 滞在する to stay, to sojourn, to remain

takaku-suru 高くする to make high or loud, to raise

teiji-suru 提示する to show, to indicate, to exhibit

teisha-suru 停車する to stop a vehicle

teishutsu-suru 提出する to submit, to present

tenji-suru 展示する to display, to exhibit

tenka-suru 点火する to set fire, to ignite

tenka-suru 添加する to add, to annex

teru-suru テルする to telephone

tesuto-suru テストする to test, to try

tobei-suru 渡米する to make a voyage to America, to travel to America

tochaku-suru 到着する to arrive, to reach

tōgō-suru 統合する to unify, to integrate

tōhyō-suru 投票する to vote, to poll, to ballot

tōjō-suru 搭乗する to embark

tokō-suru 渡航する to travel by sea, to make a voyage, to sail for

tōkō-suru 登校する to go to school, to attend school

tokubai-suru 特売する to sell at a special price

tōsan-suru 倒産する to go bankrupt

tōsen-suru 当選する to win an election, to be elected

tōsō-suru 逃走する to escape, to flee

tsūchi-suru 通知する to advise, to inform, to notify

tsuika-suru 追加する to add, to supplement

tsūka-suru 通過する to pass
tsūyō-suru 通用する to circulate, to be current

[U]
uerukamu-suru ウエルカムする to welcome
ukai-suru 迂回する to detour, to take a long way around
*ukkari-suru うっかりする to be absentminded, to be unconscious
unten-suru 運転する to operate, to drive
unzari-suru うんざりする to be bored, to be fed up

[W]
*wai-wai-suru わいわいする to be noisy

[Y]
yasu uri-suru 安売りする to bargain, to sell cheap
yoginaku-suru 余儀無くする to oblige, to compel
yōkyū-suru 要求する to request, to demand
yoshū-suru 予習する to study in preparation
yotei-suru 予定する to be scheduled, to expect, to plan
yoyaku-suru 予約する to make reservations, to reserve
*yura-yura-suru ゆらゆらする to sway, to waver

[Z]
zaijū-suru 在住する to reside, to live
zaiseki-suru 在席する to be at one's seat, to be in the office
zangyō-suru 残業する to work overtime
zōka-suru 増加する to increase, to grow